Beyond the Courthouse

By the same author

Addison County Justice

(Eriksson) Forest Dale, VT, 1997

Beyond the Courthouse

TALES OF LAWYERS AND LAWYERING

Peter Langrock

INTRODUCTION BY ROBERT F. DRINAN, S. J.

Paul S. Eriksson, *Publisher*
Forest Dale, Vermont

5 4 3 2 1

Library of Congress Cataloging-in-Publication Data

Langrock, Peter.
Beyond the courthouse: tales of lawyers and lawyering / by Peter Langrock;
introduction by Robert F. Drinan.
p.   cm.
Includes index.
ISBN 0-8397-1034-8 (cloth)
1. Law—United States Anecdotes. I. Title.
K184.L35   1999
349.73—dc21   99-38177
CIP

To my clients

CONTENTS

PREFACE

The phrase that one is "called to the bar" has always had special significance to me. I can think of no other profession that yields such a rewarding life. From the first grade on, I always wanted to be a lawyer, and I never thought seriously of any other profession. The law has been good to me, providing a constant chance for learning, all the while attempting to help people who have asked me to be their lawyer.

The fabric of the law is people. People, with their foibles and their talents, who need lawyers. Cases that go through the courts are nothing more nor less than controversies where the people involved have been unable to resolve their differences, despite the many other avenues society offers for bringing them into agreement. An important part of the law concerns those who come into the criminal justice system because society says that they have engaged in conduct for which they must be accountable to the public.

It is my hope that the readers of *Beyond the Courthouse* will think of the people involved in these stories as real people, and derive from them a perspective on the day-to-day things that have occurred in rural communities over the second half of the twentieth century. Some of the stories are truly local and others span out to unexpected surprising areas for a rural legal practice. All have counterparts that have occurred in county courthouses and lawyers' offices all across America.

I've tried to be faithful to the factual settings in which each story occurred. I hope in the telling I can convey a taste of the context in which they arose. For my contemporaries, this may invoke some nostalgia. For younger readers, I hope it imparts the flavor of some of the ways their predecessors dealt with the world.

In a courthouse in Vermont there hangs a large framed picture showing rows of individual photographs of each member of the

Vermont Bar of 1911. When I started my practice in 1960, I had the good fortune to actually work on cases with lawyers pictured in that photograph. In that same collection of photographs were lawyers who in their early years practiced law, or at least practiced with lawyers, who had been active during the Civil War. I have always been impressed by the quantity of history, with its attendant changes, that takes place in the course of a lifetime. In the law a part of history is passed on by elder lawyers to younger lawyers. A great deal of history is contained in the old state supreme court reports, which are nothing more than stories about how law has been applied to real human disputes. Other stories do not make it to the books but are passed along orally. One of the great joys of lawyering is to find yourself in the company of other trial lawyers with enforced free time, having to wait for a judge or a jury to come to a decision. It is during this time that lawyers trade stories and share their life experiences. My wish is for some of those stories to be enjoyed by a broader audience.

In my service at the bar, I have been very lucky in being able to maintain my independence. I've never had a client I couldn't afford to fire nor been in a position where I could not take on the advocacy of a particular position for fear of political considerations. Perhaps most important of all, I have been able to follow the rule I set down for myself early in the practice: never turn down a case that's fun. I hope others will share that fun in *Beyond the Courthouse*.

—Peter Langrock

INTRODUCTION

BY ROBERT F. DRINAN, S.J.
PROFESSOR, GEORGETOWN UNIVERSITY LAW CENTER

When you finish reading this fascinating collection of true stories, you will wish you had become a "country lawyer." The author, a happy practitioner for some 39 years in Vermont, has done it all! He has been a prosecutor, a defender of persons charged with crimes, and is a highly respected lawyer who spends eighty percent of his time in litigation.

The title "country lawyer" may apply to Peter Langrock, but in the book *The Best Lawyers in 1997-98*, he was placed among the best in Vermont in the areas of business litigation, criminal defense, first amendment law and personal injury litigation.

Peter Langrock also has a rich life outside of Vermont where he started to practice in 1960 after his graduation from the University of Chicago Law School. He is a life member of the National Conference of Commissioners on Uniform State Laws, an elected member of the prestigious American Law Institute, and a state delegate from Vermont to the American Bar Association. More recently he has been a member of the board of governors of the ABA.

I first met Peter in 1981 when he was the chairman of the Section of Individual Rights and Responsibilities of the American Bar Association. He was progressive and strong on all of the tough issues of civil liberties. His credibility in these controversial areas was enhanced because he was from Vermont.

In contrast to these notable achievements, Peter Langrock in *Beyond the Courthouse* tells about clients he served and the human foibles he witnessed. He writes good short stories, some of them with an O'Henry twist. The reader going through this volume should play a game by selecting the best tale in the book.

Langrock's clients run the gamut. They include speeders, farmers, drug dealers, murderers, and horse breeders. He enjoys them all but states categorically that helping apple farmers get adequate foreign labor to pick apples was "the most significant legal accomplishment of my career."

Lawyers in these fascinating stories generally live up to their noble mission. They don't overstate the evidence they possess. They don't misrepresent. They work within the adversary system but they don't present evidence they know judges should not accept.

The lawyers who are players in this engaging book make you proud to be a lawyer. They probably have the same level of showmanship most lawyers have but they seem to be less self-promoting, seem to have a sense that lawyers are not hustlers or hucksters. They are officers of the legal system, moral architects and spiritual directors.

Recent stories about lawyers are filled with grim statistics that suggest a significant percentage of attorneys are discontent or disillusioned with their chosen profession. Reading Peter Langrock's book one gets the idea lawyers in Vermont do not have this malaise. They are engaged with real people who need them in very personal and unusually distressing matters. Whether you win or lose you can feel that you use your talents and your character to get the best version of justice available.

Those who read this lovely book will be envious of their brother Peter in Vermont. Years ago he bought a home, a barn and 110 acres for $13,000! He has a life which he enjoys. But mostly he likes being a lawyer because he cherishes his independence. He says it all in these moving words in his preface:

In my service at the bar, I have been very lucky in being able to maintain my independence. I've never had a client I couldn't afford to fire nor been in a position where I could not take on the advocacy of a particular position for fear of political considerations.

Beyond the Courthouse

AUTHOR'S NOTE

*Numbered footnotes in the text indicate case citations
listed in the back on page 171.*

1.

GIBSON'S FEDERAL COURT

There are portraits of several governors in the grand room next to the House chambers in Montpelier, the room that displays Julian Stuart's mammoth oil painting of the First Vermont Brigade at the Civil War Battle of Cedar Creek. Among the portraits is one of Colonel Ernest W. Gibson, Jr.

Ernest W. Gibson, Sr. was a U.S. Senator from Vermont during most of the 1930s. Upon his death in early 1940, Ernest W. Gibson, Jr. was appointed by his good friend Governor George D. Aiken to fill out his father's term. It was commonly believed that Aiken, coming to the end of his second term as governor, would run for the U.S. Senate and that Ernest W. Gibson, Jr. would step aside, as part of a political pact. Aiken did run and was elected. Both Aiken and Gibson were Republicans. While the rest of the country was caught up in the "New Deal," it must be remembered that in the 1936 presidential election Maine and Vermont were the only states counted in the Republican column. Gibson may have been a Republican by party, but he was a populist by nature. In his short stint in the U.S. Senate, he crossed the aisle and befriended a Democrat, a senator from Missouri by the name of Harry S Truman. This friendship was later to play a major role in the history of lawyering in Vermont.

In the early summer of 1941, before the entry of the United States into World War II, young Ernest W. Gibson, Jr., an officer in the national guard, having finished his short service as a U.S. Senator, answered the call of his country. In July of 1943, while fighting in the South Pacific, Gibson suffered a head wound during a Japanese air raid. Fortunately, the strafer's bullet did not penetrate his skull but left a large gash in his scalp. Scalp wounds bleed profusely, and shortly thereafter, pictures of former U.S. Senator Ernest Gibson, Jr., with his bloody head bandages, were carried by newspapers across the country.

Gibson quickly rose to the rank of colonel. In late 1944, as hostilities wound down, he was assigned to the Pentagon. Upon Roosevelt's death in 1945, when Truman became President and commander in chief of the U.S. military, there were those in the Pentagon who didn't believe Truman should be their boss, and in their distrust of the former haberdasher from Missouri, they were not always candid nor open with him. Gibson became a strong link in getting information from the Pentagon to the President. Their friendship grew. When World War II ended, Gibson returned home to Brattleboro. He made a run for governor and took on the powerful Republican machine, a conservative group of Republicans headed by Mortimer Proctor. In a hard-fought primary election in the late summer of 1946, the handsome, dashing war hero, campaigning around the state in a white palm beach suit, upset the machine and won the Republican nomination for governor. In 1946 this was tantamount to election, and in November, Ernest W. Gibson, Jr. was duly elected Governor of the State of Vermont. Gibson, as governor, and his old friend George Aiken, now U.S. Senator, ruled Vermont politics and formed what was known as the Aiken/Gibson wing of the Republican party, which was noted for their sensitivity to the people of the state. They were in fact true populists. As governor, Gibson led the campaign to change the face of law enforcement from a hodgepodge of local police departments, sheriff departments, and the Vermont highway patrol to that of a modern state police organization. He appointed another distinguished veteran of W.W. II, General Merritt Edson, to lead the Vermont State Police, which soon became the dominant police organization, with full jurisdiction throughout the state.

In 1949, in his second term as governor, probably realizing that there were limited political possibilities for an ex-governor, especially with his good friend George Aiken and the stalwart Ralph Flanders (the man who in 1955 introduced the resolution of censure against the red-baiting Joseph McCarthy of Wisconsin) serving in the U.S. Senate, he saw an opportunity which would dictate his future career. Federal Judge James Leamy died, creating a vacancy for the lone federal judgeship in Vermont. This was a position of prestige and power, and being the only federal judgeship in Vermont, it was an extremely attractive job. It also had the advantage of providing life tenure, and by Vermont's standards a good salary. It was an appointment that Gibson decided he wanted.

The problem was that he was a Republican and the federal administration was Democratic. Up through the late 50s, and finally ending with the election of Phil Hoff as Governor in 1962, the Democratic party in Vermont was more concerned with obtaining the patronage positions that would flow out of Washington and its Democratic administration than in actually getting people elected. Joseph McNamara, a distinguished member of the Vermont Bar and a Democrat, was serving as U.S. Attorney, and it was assumed by all that in due course he would be appointed the U.S. District Judge. Gibson had other plans.

The story is that he hitched a ride on a Vermont National Guard airplane to our nation's capitol and arrived at the White House virtually unannounced with a request to see his old friend from the U.S. Senate, President Harry S Truman. Truman immediately made time for a meeting with Gibson, and the conversation went something like this: Gibson: "Mr. President, It's good to see you." Truman: "Ernest, what brings you to Washington?" Gibson: "I want to be appointed the federal judge in Vermont." Truman: "Why in hell aren't you a Democrat?" Gibson: "How in hell would I get elected in Vermont if I were a Democrat?" Without further ado, Truman picked up the phone, called the U.S. Attorney General, and said, "When you recommend an appointment for the U.S. District Judge for Vermont, I want you to recommend Ernest W. Gibson, Jr." Their conversation then went on to less serious matters.

A short time later an announcement came out of Washington that President Truman, based on the recommendation of the Attorney General of the United States, had submitted to the senate the nomination of Governor Ernest W. Gibson, Jr. to be the U.S. District Judge for Vermont. This came as a surprise to the Democratic regulars in Vermont, but given Gibson's close relationship with the Republican senators from Vermont, and the fact that he himself had served in the U.S. Senate, there was little doubt but that he would be confirmed. In fact, he was confirmed and resigned his post as governor to accept the position as federal judge in January, 1950.

At the time of Gibson's appointment to the bench, the lieutenant governor was Harold Arthur. Harold had been the Master of the state Grange and was known throughout the state because of his ability to whistle. Voters in selecting a lieutenant governor were apparently less concerned about an ability to govern than they were about the talent of a virtuoso whistler. Arthur assumed the governorship, and although he served a subsequent term, he never became known as an astute executive.

AN ASIDE

Harold Arthur actually played a role in the election of the first Vermont Democrat as a congressman since the Civil War. In 1958, in a five-way race, he became the Republican nominee for the U.S. Congress under circumstances where he received barely more than twenty percent of the total popular vote in the Republican primary. In a five-way race, he barely beat out two formidable opponents, Harris Thurber, a professor of political science at Middlebury College, and Luke Crispe, one of Vermont's great trial lawyers, from Brattleboro. The press was so outraged that this highly competent whistler, but incompetent executive, could win the nomination that they endorsed his Democratic opponent, William Meyer, an unknown forester from Poultney, Vermont. Meyer pulled an upset and served as the lone congressman for Vermont from 1959 to 1961. He was unseated in the 1960 election by Bob Stafford, who had worked his way up through the Republican ranks from attorney general to lieutenant governor, and then finally governor. Meyer was a liberal who would make even Bernie Sanders, Vermont's current lone representative, an independent socialist elected first in 1990, look like a middle-of-the-roader. In 1959, at the height of the Cold War, when a vote was taken concerning a resolution to deny the admission of Red

China to the U.N., Meyer's was the sole vote in Congress against that resolution.

As a federal judge, Gibson's inherent love for the little man, and his great distrust of insurance companies, soon enshrined him among the members of the bar as a "plaintiff's" judge. Among his strongest fans was Jack Conley.

Jack Conley had come to Vermont as a student at Middlebury College and returned to Middlebury after law school. He served as state's attorney of Addison County during the late 30s and early 40s, and became one of the state's best trial lawyers. Among Jack's many abilities was his capacity to consume martinis, or at least his capacity to recover after their consumption. In 1958 there was no full-time bankruptcy judge; the bankruptcy matters in the state of Vermont were handled by lawyers who were appointed as referees in bankruptcy, a part-time job. Jack, an old friend and early supporter of Judge Gibson, was appointed a referee. The first time I met Judge Gibson was when, as Jack's law clerk, I accompanied him to the federal court in Rutland. Two down-country lawyers from New York argued an appeal from one of Conley's decisions as a referee, and the appeal was to the U.S. District Court and was to be heard by Judge Gibson. Jack and I sat in the front row of the spectator seats in the marble-paneled courtroom at the federal post office and courthouse in Rutland. It was apparent that the thrust of the New York lawyers' arguments, aside from the legal substance, was that they were upset with what they believed to be unprofessional conduct by the referee, Jack Conley. They accused Jack of being under the influence of alcohol while he had sat on their case. Judge Gibson listened to their pleas, not too patiently, and then interrupted them with a tirade: how dare they come to Vermont and accuse a referee in his court of being drunk while on the bench. He quickly sent them packing back to New York and they left the courtroom with little satisfaction. As they were leaving, the judge's secretary approached Jack and said that the judge would like to see him in chambers. I was allowed to tag along. As we walked into the chambers, Judge Gibson, with a scowl on his face, said, "Jack, you've got to stop drinking while you're on the bench."

Conley, in another case, was driving down to federal court in Rutland. This was in between the times when his driving license was suspended for DWI. Jack was carrying his file for the case, in an accordion fiber file about two inches thick. Before he unlocked his car, he laid the file on top it. He opened the door and without further ado drove away. At some point the file blew off the car, never to be seen again. When Jack got to Rutland, he realized what had happened. He was quite sure his clients would not appreciate his showing up in court without a file. His solution to the problem was to go over to Ryan, Smith & Carbine, then the largest firm in Rutland, where he asked if he could borrow a file for the afternoon. The secretary to whom he made the request asked, "What file do you want?" Jack responded, "I don't care, as long as it's in an accordion folder and about two inches thick." They accommodated him and he went into court, and after successfully arguing his motion, he returned the file. The clients were never the wiser that the file he was carrying and never opened had absolutely nothing to do with their case.

Every plaintiff's lawyer in the state, because of Judge Gibson's open concern for the injured person and his equally open hostility to insurance companies, tried to figure a way to bring any personal injury case into federal court. In the 1960s the federal court was staffed with a single court reporter by the name of Herman Vesper, who followed the judge to the several courthouses in the state. Ordinarily, at the conclusion of the plaintiff's case, defense counsel would make a motion for a directed verdict in its favor, saying that the plaintiff had failed to establish a case, and that the facts made it clear that the plain-tiff's claim was barred by the doctrine of contributory negligence. The doctrine of contributory negligence theoretically held that even if the defendant was ninety-nine percent negligent and the plaintiff only one percent negligent in causing the accident, the plaintiff was barred from recovering any money. To say the least, Judge Gibson was not friendly towards that doctrine. Judge Gibson would listen patiently while defense counsel would make their arguments, and then he would turn to the court reporter and ask him, "Herman, how should I rule on this motion?" Herman would reach down for a straw boater that he kept at his side. An addition had been made to the traditional band that circled the base of the cap, and as he placed the hat on his head, defense counsel could see the word on the band, "Denied."

When the time came to submit a case to the jury, Judge Gibson would give his charge of the law. He always technically covered the doctrine of contributory negligence, but he did it rapidly, in a low voice, with a scowl on his face. As soon as he finished, he would lapse into the part of the charge where he would remind the jury that this was the only opportunity the injured person would have to recover damages and that it was their duty in the appropriate case to give full and adequate damages for all the plaintiff had suffered, including an award for pain and suffering. A plaintiff's case brought in federal court was worth at least twice as much for settlement purposes as the same case would have been worth if it had been brought in a county court.

Lest you think that Judge Gibson's court was only a one-way street, you should know that he could also put a plaintiff in his place if he thought he was asking for too much. In the late 1960s I had been asked to come to Brattleboro to try a case for Luke Crispe. The case involved a trucker who had fallen on slippery linoleum when he was unloading some supplies at the Brattleboro Pepsi-Cola bottling plant. Luke, who had previously represented the owner of the bottling plant, felt uncomfortable personally trying the case and asked me if I would do it.

During the trial, Luke decided to sit at counsel's table, and it seemed that every time I would rise to ask a question, he would pull the bottom of my suit jacket and whisper to me exactly what he wanted asked. I managed to survive.

I also managed to survive a witness who shall remain etched in my memory forever. Our client had ruptured a disc in the accident and had undergone a spinal fusion. A spinal fusion in the late 1960s was a much more serious operation than it is today, and required as much as six weeks of complete bed rest in the hospital following the surgery. The problem in our case was that when our client had first injured his back, instead of seeking out an orthopedic surgeon, he had gone to a chiropractor. While the chiropractor had little to offer about the extent of the injuries, we needed him to show the connection between the fall at the Pepsi-Cola plant and the back injury. It was important to show that the client had immediately sought medical help from the chiropractor. The chiropractor arrived late and I had to call him to the stand without having a chance to talk to him. He wore a clip-on red bow tie and was chewing gum. He was supposed to bring his records, including any x-rays he had taken. He testified from his single page of medical records which mentioned he had indeed taken x-rays. When I asked about the x-rays, he explained he had put them in a pile of x-rays in the basement of his home and that they were lost when shortly before the trial he had moved to a new office. To this day I have a mental image of him wearing a beanie cap with a propeller, but I know that didn't happen — or did it?

Despite the problems I had with this witness, I felt we had a good case and I wanted it to go to the jury. On the afternoon of the second day of trial Charles Ryan, who was defending the Pepsi-Cola Bottling Company, made an offer of $8,500 to settle the case. Ryan was one of the true giants of the Vermont bar, a fairminded and sensitive insurance defense lawyer, and in the best meaning of the word, a gentleman. I communicated that offer to my client, and recommended that we reject it and continue with the trial. Luke Crispe disagreed. He thought that considering all the factors in the case, it should be settled at the $8,500 figure. He held back nothing in telling me and our mutual client just that. By this time, the client had spent a great deal of time working with me in the preparation of his case and he was determined to follow my recommendation.

I was talking with our client in one of the attorney's rooms when a summons came from chambers. In chambers were Judge Gibson, Charlie Ryan, and my co-counsel, Luke Crispe. The judge turned to me and said, "Mr. Langrock, I understand Mr. Ryan has made an offer in this case of $8,500." I responded that in fact he had, but that I thought it was inadequate based upon the injuries and the way I felt the case was going in. At this point, Judge Gibson indicated that Mr. Ryan had also told him that some twenty years earlier our client had filed a workers' compensation claim (then workman's compensation) for a back injury, but yet when he was deposed in this case, he indicated he had never previously hurt his back. Gibson suggested quite strongly he thought the $8,500 was an appropriate figure, and he would hate to see my client take the stand and be in the position of perjuring himself. I looked at the judge and said, "I think I understand the message quite clearly." I went back to my client and told him we had just settled the case for $8,500, explaining the circumstances to him. My client, realizing the predicament of his own making, quickly acquiesced. Both Luke and Charlie were pleased. I had been taught that a cocky young lawyer had to temper his approach in light of the less formal and powerful old-boy network of my seniors.

Judge Gibson had a pretty good idea of what a case was worth, and during the course of a trial he kept abreast of negotiations. He would push reticent defense counsel into paying what he thought a case was worth. He had even been known to insist counsel get the insurance company claims manager to the court so he could tell him what he thought of the situation. He also would try to protect inept or young plaintiffs' lawyers. In one of my early plaintiff's trials in federal court, opposing counsel was Albert Coffrin, later to become federal judge. We had a good case, but Coffrin would not meet my demand with what I considered a reasonable response. He got me into a position of bargaining against myself with my demand coming down step-by-step, while he did not move from his position. This went on for about two days, and Gibson, knowing the status of the negotiations, called me to chambers and said, "You've come down far enough." He then told Al Coffrin to go out and make a call to the insurance company. We settled at exactly the point Judge Gibson thought was fair.

In the Town of Middlebury, as you go up Merchants Row and meet South Pleasant Street, you will see the old Town Hall. The building was constructed in 1884 as an opera house. It was designed by Clinton Smith, the same architect who designed the Addison County Courthouse, just one hundred yards or so away, across the old county square park. They are both constructed of red brick, and when examined, the similarities are apparent. A casual visitor to Middlebury might not make the connection, as there lies between them the white clapboard Gamaliel Painter home which was constructed eighty–four years earlier.

The main portion of the Town Hall is located slightly above ground level and originally featured a large theatre with a balcony facing the stage located across the end of the hall. During the 1940s and 50s, Ken Gorham rented the building from the town and ran competition to The Campus movie theatre located on Main Street, showing movies in "The Town Hall Theatre." In the summer months outside in front of the theatre was a Dairy Queen soft ice cream stand.

By the late 1950s television had made its inroad into the movie theatre business and the Town Hall Theatre closed. The town clerk's office, which had been located on the floor under the main auditorium at the back of the building, was moved to the old high school which was newly renovated after having suffered a major fire. A new union high school had been built at the south end of Court Street, and with the municipal functions moved into the refurbished old Middlebury high school building, the old Town Hall was put up for sale.

Sam Emilo, entrepreneur about town, purchased the building for ten thousand dollars. Some years later he sold it to the Knights of Columbus to serve as their meeting and function rooms. (In the late 1990's, there began a movement to purchase the building for a community art and business center and restore it to the magnificence of its days as an opera house.)

Shortly after Emilo purchased the building, the huge brass bell, cast in 1884, that hung in its tower was on its way to the scrap metal dealer. A couple of local citizens, Arthur Healy, a well-known watercolor artist and professor at Middlebury College, and Theron Wolcott, a Middlebury contractor, raised money to reimburse Emilo for the scrap value of the bell. They had it trucked to the Sheldon Museum, where it sits today in the courtyard. During the time that Sam Emilo owned the building, he rented out the main floor to a family-run bar and restaurant business. The Derochers, who ran the business, named the operation the Belmont.

Although I personally liked Sam Emilo, the feelings were not fully reciprocated. I had prosecuted Sam along with a local attorney, Wayne Bosworth, in a usury scam early in my tenure as state's attorney, and although Sam was acquitted, he never forgave me for prosecuting him.

There were two entrances to the Belmont restaurant, one through the front door, but the one most often used was a side door that opened onto South Pleasant Street. There were six wooden steps from the ground to the doorway where there was a small platform which was lit at night by a single bare bulb. This was the same entrance that I used when I stopped by after work to have a beer or two with a shot of cognac on the side. If the libation seems to indicate that there was a strong French-Canadian influence among those who patronized the bar, that surmise would be correct.

Darrell LaFlam was the father of eleven children and lived on the Blake Roy Road near the Salisbury/Middlebury line. One night Darrell LaFlam visited the Belmont. As the owners turned off the outside lights indicating closing time, Darrell finished his last drink and left by the side door. It was a dark night and with the single bulb turned off, there was little light on the steps. Darrell stumbled, fell down the steps, and hit his head. He died ten days later as a result of complications stemming from the head injury.

His widow came to see me and I initiated a wrongful death action against both the Belmont restaurant, the operating corporation, and the owner of the building, Sam Emilo. Bob Erdmann, of the Wick, Dinse & Allen law firm, appeared on behalf of the Belmont, Inc., and Jimmy Haugh, perhaps the greatest insurance defense lawyer of his era, from the law firm of Ryan, Smith & Carbine in Rutland, entered the case on behalf of Sam Emilo. In order for the widow to prevail against the restaurant, it had to be shown that the restaurant was negligent having turned out the light on the steps prior to the last patron leaving, and that the bad lighting was a cause of the accident. I had concentrated on that part of the claim as it seemed the strongest from a legal standpoint.

On the other hand, in order to hold Emilo liable, it had to be proven that the design of the steps and the attendant lighting were defective. We also had to show that Emilo had retained control of those steps as the landlord, rather than surrendering control over the entrance to the operator of the restaurant. This was a much tougher matter to prove.

The case came to trial in the federal courthouse in Montpelier before Judge Gibson. After the jury was drawn and we started the trial, Bob Erdmann came to me and said that his client had only five thousand dollars worth of insurance coverage and that the company was willing to pay the five thousand dollars to settle their portion of the case. There was little option but to accept that figure, as the corporation had no assets, other than some silverware, glasses, and a few tables and chairs. We were disappointed, as we had expected that there was more liability coverage than the five thousand dollars, and certainly the case had a far greater potential value.

After Mr. Erdmann and the restaurant were excused from the proceeding, the trial continued against Sam Emilo alone. Jimmy Haugh had prepared his client to testify that when he leased the building, he had leased the entire operation, including the steps, and that he had not retained in any way any control over the outside entranceway.

Sometimes your past sins, if drinking cognac shots with beer chasers is a sin, come back not to haunt you, but to help you. Sam Emilo was called to the stand. He was antagonistic from the start, even through the preliminary questions. Judge Gibson admonished him to just answer the questions, but Sam knew better.

When I asked, "Are you familiar with the back entranceway to the Belmont restaurant?" Sam glowered and said, "I'm not as familiar with it as you are. I see you going in there all the time." The next question: "That is your building, is it not? You did build the entranceway on the building at the side door, didn't you?" Sam's response, "Of course I did." This was quickly followed with, "And, of course, you kept control of those steps, didn't you?" Sam, forgetting all the admonitions of his counsel and following his course of wanting to put me down rather than to think of what he was saying, said, "Of course I did." I stopped with, "No more questions," and a recess was called. During the recess Jimmy Haugh made a call to his insurance company and was able to get authority to make an offer of an additional payment of seven thousand five hundred dollars. We settled the case.

AN ASIDE

In retrospect, the amount of settlement seems very small by today's standards. It must, however, be put in the perspective of the values at that time, when a dollar and a half per hour was the standard wage for a carpenter; ten dollars per hour was the standard charge for a lawyer; and my wife and I had been able to purchase our first home of one hundred and ten acres, a house in excellent condition and a small barn, for thirteen thousand dollars.

2.

THE MILK STRIKE HOMICIDE

Homicides were not commonplace in Vermont in the 1950s and
60s. From 1958, when I started my clerkship in the law offices
of Conley Foote & Underwood, through the end of my tenure in
1965 as Addison County's state's attorney, no murders occurred in
the county. Murder cases that did take place became causes célèbres
and were followed closely by newspapers throughout the state. When
lawyers get together, they talk about cases of the past. One of these
cases was told to me in bits and pieces by Ralph Foote, who was lieutenant governor of Vermont from 1960 to 1964. He knew of the case
only secondhand, as it involved the great milk strike in 1941, long
before he was admitted to practice law. He learned about it from his
partner, Jack Conley, who had been the state's attorney of Addison
County at the time. The case was defended by Jim Donoway and
Harold O'Brien, both legends of the bar.

My only knowledge of Jim Donoway is from word of mouth,
although I have a strong visual image of him as captured in a watercolor
portrait by an art professor at Middlebury College, Arthur Healy. The
picture showing his large jowls and bright eyes hung in the judge's

chambers of the old courthouse. One story I heard about Donoway concerned the time when a local man who sold meat from the back of his truck approached Donoway on the street. The vendor told him about cutting a piece of meat on the tailgate of his truck and taking it into a house. While he was there, a neighbor's dog stole the remaining part of the cut of meat off the tailgate. He asked Donoway whether the owner of that dog was liable for the cost of the meat. Donoway pondered a moment and said, "In my opinion the law is quite clear that the owner is responsible to you for the reasonable value of the meat." The vendor continued, "That's good, Mr. Donoway, because it was your dog, and you owe me one dollar." Jim Donoway took a silver dollar from his pocket and handed it to the vendor without another word. The next day the vendor received a letter from Jim Donoway enclosing a bill for two dollars for professional services and advice rendered.

Harold O'Brien had died before I started practice. He had been known as the best trial lawyer in Vermont. Alma Sherwin, who was the clerk of the Addison County Court when I was first admitted to the bar, told me he always came to court with a fresh flower as a boutonniere in his lapel. His partner, Edwin Lawrence, was the lawyer for the then powerful Rutland Railroad. I have visual images in my mind of both of these men from photographs that hang in the lawyers' room in the Rutland County Courthouse.

Jack Conley I knew well, and not just from legend or pictures. I started my clerkship under him and, when I was state's attorney, I crossed swords with him many times in cases where he was the defense counsel. Jack, after leaving his position as state's attorney in the 40s, went into private practice and became a hard-hitting protector of the ordinary citizen, following in the tradition of his opponents in the milk strike case. All of these men were my mentors, one in actuality and two in spirit. The story of the milk strike homicide fascinated me.

On June 30, 1941, more than one thousand dairy farmers attended a meeting at the New Haven Town Hall. (To put this number in perspective, the total population of New Haven in 1941 was only 881 and in all of Vermont today there are only about 1,700 active dairy farms.) The farmers were responding to a call from the Dairy Farmers Union for a milkshed-wide milk holiday to begin on July 1 in support of a demand for a flat minimum milk price of three dollars per hundredweight. They argued that with the rising costs of doing business, Vermont family farms could not survive on the then existing milk prices. This meant dumping milk rather than sending it to market.

The meeting was chaired by a Bridport farmer, Wade Walker. Another of the organizers, Donald Downs of Cornwall, spoke: "We're trying to conduct the milk holiday peacefully — we've simply refused to let the purchasers set the price for us. We as producers have our own idea of what the price should be in order for us to live." A vote was taken and only twenty-three of the assembled farmers opposed the holiday.

In 1941 there were no bulk tanks in Vermont; milk was delivered in cans to the creameries located along the Rutland Railroad, to be shipped to the city markets by rail. The first day of the strike was effective. In Middlebury only six cans out of the usual five to six hundred were delivered. New Haven deliveries consisted of only ninety out of about six hundred cans, and Salisbury had only seven out of a usual six hundred cans. Vergennes farmers were less supportive of the holiday, and seventy-two cans were delivered, the usual expectation being two hundred and fifty.

On Wednesday, the 2nd of July, there were several episodes of striking farmers stopping trucks taking milk to the creamery. After stopping the trucks, the striking farmers emptied the milk cans onto the ground. While there had not been any serious incidents, the sheriff of Addison County, Ralph Sweet, decided to assign deputies to farmers who wanted to break through the picket lines and deliver their milk. One of these deputies was Ray Russell. On July 4, Russell was asked to accompany the truck of Sanford Derrick of Waltham through the picket lines. Derrick's milk had been dumped from his truck the previous day. On that Friday, Russell accompanied Derrick trying to take milk to the Vergennes plant. The truck was halted in front of a line of farmers who had set up a roadblock. Deputy Russell got off the truck and told the men to disperse. He got back on the running board as the truck started up. The farmers who blocked the truck were not pleased to see a "scab" trying to run the picket line. Four of them jumped on to the truck and started to dump the cans of milk. Russell tried to stop the dumping, and in the course of the altercation, he was hit on the head, fell off the truck, and lay unconscious on the ground. He died within the hour.

Four farmers, George and William Sullivan of Panton, Donald O'Donnell of Panton, and Martin Pilger of Waltham were charged with manslaughter by State's Attorney Jack Conley. Jim Donoway initially appeared on behalf of the four defendants. Shortly thereafter the Dairy Farmers Union hired Harold O'Brien of Rutland to assist as co-counsel. At the arraignment the municipal judge was George Farr, known to most of his friends as "Punk" Farr. Punk, although he had never been admitted to law school, served as sheriff of the county, municipal judge, and county clerk, and continued to serve as deputy clerk well into his eighties, until his death in the early 1960s. The municipal court had jurisdiction only over preliminary matters and so all four men were bound over to the county court for grand jury proceedings. Judge Farr set bail at twenty-five hundred dollars per man. With the help of friends and neighbors, the four farmers were able to raise that sum and each of them was released. A grand jury was quickly convened and indictments were returned charging each of the defendants with manslaughter.

Emotions were running high in the county. There was a great deal of sympathy for the farmers and the milk strike, and the general belief was that what happened was an accident and not a crime.

The state, recognizing that it had a potential problem if the cases were to be tried in Addison County, did the unusual thing by asking for a change of venue. Almost always a change of venue is requested by defendants who claim local feelings or adverse publicity would prejudice the jury against them. Conley and Donoway, who were good friends, got into an angry and personal exchange in the courtroom. Donoway criticized Conley as to affidavits that Conley had filed in connection with the motion, and Conley quickly countered that it was Donoway's brother-in-law, Roland T. Robinson of Ferrisburgh, who had first signed an affidavit for the defense. Judge Charles B. Adams, recognizing the rising tensions, quickly interceded, calmed both attorneys down, and struck their heated exchange from the official court record. This was on the 21st of August. Judge Adams then denied the state's petition for a change of venue and set a trial for October 14th, a little over three months after the incident.

The four defendants would be tried together, and in October on the scheduled trial date a jury of twelve men was selected. The jurors Robert Hayes, Goshen; Linus Needham, Whiting; Deacy Leonard, Shoreham; E. B. Barber, Bristol; C. H. Ellis, Salisbury; Henry Dike, Starksboro; Bancroft Brown, Hancock; Wilfred Brown, Bristol; Carl C. Swinington, Leicester; C. L. Needham, Whiting; Ray Gill, Cornwall; George Kidder, Middlebury, all had surnames tracing back to

Vermont's earliest settlers. The demographics of the community were such that the jury included seven dairy farmers, one apple farmer, one house painter, one laborer, one accountant, and one businessman. As was the custom of the time, the jurors were sequestered for the duration of the trial and were housed at the Middlebury Inn at state expense.

AN ASIDE

In 1941, women were not legally qualified for jury service. On March 11, 1941, the General Assembly passed Act No. 31 to change that law. The act called for a statewide referendum on the question of whether women should be allowed to serve as jurors. If the referendum vote was yes, women would be eligible as of February 1, 1943. If the vote was no, they would still become eligible but not until February 1, 1947. The legislation contained the explanatory note when setting up the procedures for the referendum, "Those in favor of women jury service vote 'Yes' in the square above opposite the word 'Yes.' Those opposed to women jury service vote 'No' in the square above opposite the word 'No." In November of 1942 the "Yeses" prevailed over the "Nos" by 34,982 to 20,065.

During the trial, Dr. Whitney, the state pathologist, testified that Russell had died of shock and internal hemorrhage, caused when his right ribs were crushed and his lungs and liver were punctured. His right arm was fractured, and he had a bump behind his right ear, which had been caused either by his head being struck or by its striking some object. There was testimony concerning one of the defendants on the truck having a blackjack.

The defense was based largely on lack of evidence. No one admitted seeing any specific person hit Deputy Russell. Both Donoway and O'Brien argued that Deputy Sheriff Russell had probably been thrown from the moving truck accidentally during the course of the altercation.

Jack Conley closed his final argument: "No free people can remain free if they permit violence to take precedence over law, whether it be the law of God or of man." Donoway's and O'Brien's arguments were limited to criticizing the quantity and quality of the state's evidence.

The judge charged the jury on the law and told them that if the defendants had entered into an unlawful combination prior to boarding the truck and that if this unlawful combination proximately culminated in causing Russell's death, the jury could find all of them guilty of involuntary manslaughter, even though only one of them had actually pushed Russell off the truck.

The trial covered eight days and the case was submitted to the jury for deliberations late in the afternoon of October 23. The next day, October 24, at 5:25 p.m., the courthouse bell rang announcing that the jury had reached a verdict. A large number of spectators gathered in the second floor courtroom to hear the jury announce its verdict. As the charges were read by the clerk, the foreman of the jury responded with a verdict of guilty as to involuntary manslaughter against each of the defendants.

In returning its verdict, the jury, which included the seven dairy farmers, resisted the temptation to acquit, which would have been a popular verdict, and did their duty on the facts. However, the jury did something else which was extraordinary. They went beyond simply finding the defendants guilty. After the verdicts were announced, the foreman made a statement saying that the jury was making a unanimous request that each of the four defendants be treated with mercy.

Jack Conley had taken on the unpopular cause of prosecuting four men who, in participating in the strike, were doing what they believed to be right by trying to protect the farmers and their need to make a living at farming. The jury had done its job in following the law and did so despite strong feelings that what had happened was unfortunate and unintended. The judge, taking heed of the jury's plea for mercy, followed through with a sentencing that incorporated those very themes. He fined two of the defendants four hundred dollars each and the other two defendants three hundred dollars each. As an alternative sentence, they were ordered to spend two days in jail for each dollar not paid. The fines were paid.

Today, if a law enforcement officer were killed while acting in the line of duty, I expect we would be hearing calls for imprisonment for life or for a revival of capital punishment. The moderation and the overall sense of responsibility shared by the prosecutor, defense counsel, the jury, and the judge might well serve as an example of how we today should treat happenings with unintended results.

3.

REPEAT BUSINESS

R epeat clients are not what a criminal defense lawyer is looking for. However, anyone who has ever practiced criminal defense law in a small community has soon learned that there are some people who seem to be addicted to doing things outside legal channels. They not only become repeat clients, but they become a source of referral for their friends of similar persuasions. Roy Girard was a prime example.

The first time I represented Roy Girard he was involved in a criminal charge arising from a bad check cashed at a store in Bristol. Roy had been the driver of a car with two other men accompanying him in the front seat. He pulled up in front of a store in Bristol, and Bernard Woodmansee, sitting in the middle, handed the check to a third man, who went into the store and cashed it.

During the course of the trial, the state called as a witness the man who had actually cashed the check. He had already been convicted of the charge. The state asked the usual preliminary questions, "What is your name?" He gave his name. "What is your occupation?" He responded, "professional thief."

On cross-examination he testified that he did not think Roy Girard knew the check was a bogus check. My defense of Girard was based on the theory the state had failed to prove Roy knew that the check that had been cashed was bogus. In illustrating this matter to the jury, I used three paper cups to demonstrate the relative positions of the parties in the front seat of the car. I pointed out that guilt obviously attached to the cup on the far right, representing the man who cashed the check. It could possibly extend to the second cup, which was Woodmansee, who had given him the check, but there was no evidence connecting it to the third cup, Mr. Girard, who was simply the driver. Moving the three paper cups on the table in front of the jury, I suddenly had the image of myself as a street corner performer plying the old shell game. Roy was acquitted.

Within a few months of his acquittal, Roy was charged with the burglary of a meat market and grocery store located between Morrisville and Hyde Park. This trial was held in the county courthouse in Hyde Park, the county seat of Lamoille County. Roy had been released on bail of fifteen hundred dollars and was free pending trial. The state's case was built around the testimony of a young man who had admitted participating in the burglary and claimed Roy Girard had been with him. Roy came to me saying he was being framed, that he had not participated in the burglary, but in fact was at home with some friends playing Monopoly on the night the burglary took place. He claimed the state's key witness had been given a sweetheart deal for his participation in the crime in return for implicating Girard. Despite persistent questioning, Roy did not change his position at all, and thus we were headed for trial.

By some oversight, the state had failed to get the key witness's story under oath. On the very day the trial began, this witness was taken to the sheriff's office in a building adjacent to the courthouse, and there for the first time signed under oath a statement that Roy Girard had in fact accompanied him in the burglary. At the trial we maintained that the statement of the state's key witness was false and was given in order to get a favorable deal after he had been caught in connection with the burglary.

Doreen, Roy's girlfriend, testified that he was in Burlington in his apartment with her playing Monopoly at the time of the burglary. Another young man (who later played a role as the state's chief prosecution witness in a case against Bernard Woodmansee) was there also. When called to the stand, he testified he had been in the military service in which he had been a chaplain's assistant, and that Roy Girard was telling the truth when he said he was playing Monopoly. He knew because he had been there with him. He even testified that Roy had won the game because of his acquisition of Park Place and Boardwalk. Despite his experience as a former army chaplain, I had some reservations about his testimony, but I was not in the position to substitute my judgment as to the veracity of a witness for what was ultimately the jury's determination.

Bill Keefe, an assistant attorney general, cross-examined this witness and was beginning to get under his skin just a little bit. I foresaw the potential of a complete breakdown of the witness and his story, and my doubts about his veracity were rekindled. Bill Keefe completed his cross-examination before the catastrophe happened, and I quickly rested my case. The court gave the legal charge to the jury and appointed one of the jurors as foreman, a retired army colonel. Apparently, the foreperson and the eleven other jurors accepted the credibility of the alibi witness, perhaps because of his previous career as an assistant army chaplain, and they reached a verdict of not guilty.

Roy had paid me a retainer in the case, but still owed me seven hundred and fifty dollars at the completion of the trial. We went to the clerk's office to obtain a return of the fifteen hundred dollars held as bail. Roy authorized the clerk to draw two checks, one of which was for the seven hundred and fifty dollars that he owed me. I took Roy aside and said, "Roy, so far you have led a charmed life. In less than a year you have been acquitted by juries on two felony charges, each one of which could have resulted in your doing a long time in jail. That does not happen very often. The police don't like that, and they are not going to give you any room at all. Leave Vermont, go someplace else, take Doreen with you, and start a new life. Here you will always be suspected of being part of the criminal element, and you will be associating with friends who will get you in trouble." My speech was delivered in a friendly, but authoritative tone, and was really meant to try to get Roy to think about turning over a new leaf. He looked at me for a moment before responding, "Pete, what you say makes a lot of sense. I think I'll do just that. I've got a couple of matters I've got to clear up, but then I think I'll take Doreen and leave the state." He paused a second, and then added, "Pete, you know I've always been able to pay you whenever I've gotten in trouble. Sometime I might not be able to pay you right off. Can I consider you on a retainer basis?"

So much for trying to change the spots on a leopard.

Bernard Woodmansee had a long record starting with his days as a juvenile offender. He had spent much of his adult life behind bars. In jail he settled in very well, and developed substantial notoriety as a jailhouse lawyer. In fact, as a jailhouse lawyer, he was a good one. I used to keep a file entitled, "Miscellaneous Woodmansee Motions." When I couldn't think of a "viable defense" and was desperate for an idea, I would riffle through that file, sometimes with success.

A time came when Bernard Woodmansee was finally indicted as a habitual offender in Franklin County. The habitual offender charge was a precursor of the currently in vogue legislation, three strikes and you're out. It provided that a person with a lengthy criminal record could be found to be a habitual criminal and sentenced to life in prison. The charge centered around Woodmansee and two other individuals scheming to pass some bad checks. The particular check involved in the indictment was in the amount of one hundred and twenty-five dollars and had been cashed at a bank in St. Albans. As a possible consequence of cashing this bad check was life imprisonment, it was a matter to be taken seriously. Judge William Hill asked me if I would take an assignment of the case and represent Woodmansee. This was before the public defender system was created. I accepted the assignment and a day was set for his arraignment. "Woody" was taken to St. Albans from the prison at Windsor, where he was serving time for an unrelated offense. I met with him in the small room reserved for attorneys and clients, located at the rear of the second floor courtroom in the courthouse near the top of the stairs. Woodmansee was perhaps the most notorious of the "criminal element" that was in and out of Vermont jails. His usual attorney had been John Harrington. John had been disbarred after having been convicted of extortion.[1] At our first meeting in the attorneys' room, near the entrance to the superior courtroom in St. Albans, I sat down and talked with

Woodmansee. I opened the conversation by saying, "Bernard, you know that I have never represented you before, but I have heard from a lot of sources as to your past activities. I want you to know that, unlike Harrington, I play by the rules. Just because I'm representing you does not mean I in any way approve of your actions. However, I will do my best to defend you in this case." Bernard looked at me, and he said, "Good, Pete, we're both professionals."

The modus operandi alleged by the State was that Woodmansee had made out a check and given it to an individual who went into the bank to cash it. The individual had met with the bank officer, who okayed it and cashed it. When the check was returned as forged, the police investigated, and the trail eventually led to Woodmansee. There were three persons involved in the check cashing scheme, Woodmansee who was supposed to have provided the check and supposed to have made it out, a second person who supplied the transportation, and a third person who actually went into the bank and cashed it. The driver of the car, who had turned state's evidence, incriminated Woodmansee. He was the person who had testified as the alibi witness in Girard's burglary trial when Girard claimed to have been playing Monopoly. Knowing that this individual might not be the best of witnesses, the state decided to bolster its case by hiring Elizabeth McCarthy, a noted handwriting expert from Boston. They did this at the last minute, and it wasn't until after trial started that I actually got the reports from Ms. McCarthy. I moved to exclude her as a witness, but the court said she could testify if the state would produce her for a deposition the night before she was to take the stand.

At the end of the second day of trial, we gathered at a back room in the courthouse for the deposition. Responding to my questions, Ms. McCarthy waxed eloquent about the handwriting on the back of the check. The check was allegedly endorsed by a man named Donald Griffin, and below the signature was an address in free-flowing handwriting, "RFD, Colchester, Vermont." Ms. McCarthy testified that she had had the opportunity to examine previous examples of Bernard Woodmansee's handwriting. In fact, she said she had done it so many times, she felt that she knew his handwriting quite well. She explained that, while she thought that he might have written "Donald Griffin," she couldn't be absolutely sure. However, as to the "RFD, Colchester, Vermont," there was no doubt in her mind that that was written by Bernard Woodmansee. She pointed to angles, curls, and special characteristics of the handwriting that she compared to exemplars of known samples of Woodmansee's handwriting, and said they proved conclusively in her mind that he had written "RFD, Colchester, Vermont" on the back of the check. I was somewhat skeptical, but I had neither the resources nor the time to hire a handwriting expert on behalf of Woodmansee. My only hope was to break down her testimony by cross-examination.

The next day I confronted Bernard with what she had testified to in her deposition, and he told me he might have forged the name of "Donald Griffin," but he certainly didn't write "RFD, Colchester, Vermont."

Thursday morning we arrived at court to watch the grand spectacle of Ms. McCarthy taking the stand. She wore a flowing blue dress and a matching hat, and her affectations matched her Vassar education. Bill Keefe, from the attorney general's office, whose usual job was to prosecute murder cases, was prosecuting this case because of the potential life sentence involved. His job was relatively easy. All he had to do was ask her name and what she had done in this case, and allow her to tell the jury her conclusions. With all the flair of an experienced expert witness, she went on to explain to the jury that she concluded Bernard probably, but not conclusively, had written "Donald Griffin" on the check. She was absolutely sure, however, the "RFD, Colchester, Vermont" written on the back of the check was in Woodmansee's handwriting. During my cross-examination, I tried to throw some doubt on her testimony, bringing up the amount of money the state was paying her to testify to this conclusion and the fact that she had been a favorite of the state in previous prosecutions for bad checks. I also attempted to make some inroads into her substantive testimony as well. She was a tough cookie, and although I was convinced she was talking smoke and mirrors, I was not sure the jury was likewise convinced.

Things changed. Ms. McCarthy left the stand and the bank officer who had approved the check took the stand. The witnesses were sequestered, which meant they were kept out of the courtroom and could neither hear nor were they allowed to talk about other testimony. I started questioning the banker concerning the endorsements on the back of the check. To my surprise, he said that he couldn't recall who had signed "Donald Griffin," but that he was quite sure that the "RFD, Colchester, Vermont" was in his own handwriting. I immediately took a yellow pad and asked him to write three times "RFD, Colchester, Vermont." He did so, and to the layperson's eye, it was identical to the "RFD, Colchester, Vermont" on the back of the check. So much for the smoke and mirrors of Elizabeth McCarthy.

After court that day, Bill Keefe and I, with a couple of other people, including Ms. McCarthy, retired to the Cornerstone Restaurant to discuss the day's happenings. Over cocktails, I suggested to Ms. McCarthy that maybe she made a mistake based upon the handwriting exemplar I had obtained from the bank officer in open court. She said that was very interesting, and would I mind sending it to her at her home laboratory for further examination. I agreed to do so after extracting a promise from her that she would get back to me with her conclusions. I sent her the material, but, not unsurprisingly, she never got back to me.

While this put a big crimp in the state's case, it certainly didn't end it. The next day, Friday, the state called several witnesses who testified briefly and then called their clean-up witness, the snitch. The snitch took the stand, and Bill Keefe carefully led him through the entire progression of his involvement and Woodmansee's alleged involvement in the charge. I started my cross-examination and was about halfway through it when the day came to an end and we were told to return on Monday morning.

As this case carried a possible sentence of life imprisonment, the jury had been sequestered since the beginning of the trial, and were taken back to their motel for the weekend. On Monday morning I returned to court expecting to continue my cross-examination of the state's chief witness. On arriving at court, Bill Keefe suggested that we talk to see if we could dispose of this case by a plea agreement. I said I was willing to listen, and we started some serious negotiations. I soon realized that the state's chief witness, whose cross-examination I had commenced on Friday, had skipped town, and the state was in a real pickle. I explained this to my client, and while this left us in very good shape, we were still risking the fact that the witness might be found and that Woodmansee still might be convicted of a charge which could result in a life sentence. At the time of the trial, Bernard had about eighteen months more to serve on a three-to-five year sentence on another criminal charge. He told me he would plead guilty in this case if the sentence would be no more than one year to be served concurrently with his existing sentence. This would mean that although he would rack up another felony on his record, he would not do a single extra day in jail, and even more important, would avoid the risk of a life sentence.

The judge, Franklin Billings, then a superior judge, later the chief justice of the Vermont Supreme Court, and still later a federal district judge for the District of Vermont, was apprised of the fact that the state's chief witness was now missing, and he entered into our negotiations. He would have to agree to any plea bargain we struck. Bill Keefe started with an offer of ten years instead of life. When I said this was unacceptable, it was soon reduced to five years, and then reduced further to three years of additional time. I talked to my client, who refused to budge from the one year concurrent sentence. I explained my client's position to both Bill Keefe and the judge in chambers, and as the day progressed and the witness had not been found, Keefe was left with the choice of either getting a conviction on Woodmansee's terms or having the case dismissed. Reluctantly, Keefe agreed to Woodmansee's terms, as did the judge, and the matter was disposed of in mid-afternoon by a plea of guilty and a sentence of one year to serve, concurrent with the sentence that Woodmansee was already serving. I am sure Rumpole of the Bailey would have appreciated Woodmansee's assertion that he was a professional and also his fortitude in holding out until he got the disposition that he wanted.

AN ASIDE

I have a personal recollection of the case. As I left the courthouse through the side door and came around onto the street in front of the green, the jury, having lived together for eight days, were all on the front steps saying their "goodbyes." One of the jurors saw me and said, "Mr. Langrock, would you please come here?" I walked over to where the jury was gathering, not knowing what to expect. The juror smiled at me, and said, "We just wanted to let you know we enjoyed your ties." My wife, Joann, makes all my ties, and they are both unusual and fun, and that part of the story is repeated oftentimes when I receive compliments on ties she has made.

Rumpole would have appreciated as well the cast of characters in the case when U.S. District Court Judge Bernard Leddy appointed me to defend Calvin Trudo. Trudo was charged with a bank robbery that took place in Burlington on Christmas eve of 1969. My client and two brothers, George and Josh Tatro, were alleged to have gone into the Merchants Bank branch located just off Patchen Road, wearing ski masks, carrying guns, and demanding money. The government attempted to prove they had fled the bank with a large amount of cash, gotten into a getaway car, and disappeared into the Christmas festivities. Sometime that spring when the snow had melted, a number of ski masks were found outside the Rooster Tail restaurant, about a quarter mile from the bank. A barmaid told the authorities that the Tatro brothers, whom she knew well, and Trudo, whom she identified from a picture, had come into the restaurant on Christmas Eve. This aided the investigation, and finally the Tatro brothers and my client were indicted.

The government never got enough evidence to indict the person they believed to be the driver of the getaway car, although they suggested it was Roy Girard.

At trial, the evidence showed that George Tatro had held a revolver pointed in the general direction of the tellers, as the others gathered the money. The employees, as well as the bank customers, were told to remain where they were and not to make any movements until five minutes after the masked men had left. George Tatro, who was the tallest of the group, looking through his ski mask at one of the tellers who was obviously frightened to death (actually frightened to the point where she wet herself), said, "Don't worry, just relax, nobody's gonna get hurt." At the trial she testified that his voice was actually quite reassuring, despite the circumstances. Nobody got hurt. The robbers escaped without any eyewitness identification and the FBI carried on its investigation.

All three defendants were tried together. I acted as lead-off defense counsel, being followed by Doug Pierson, who represented George Tatro, and Bill Knight, who represented Josh Tatro. The trial attorneys for the government were George Cook, the U.S. attorney, and David Gibson, an assistant U.S. attorney.

Originally, the government's case was quite thin, based solely on circumstantial evidence. It relied heavily on evidence that George Tatro had appeared at a poker game shortly after the robbery with a large quantity of one hundred dollar bills. The government's case improved shortly before the trial began when a crucial piece of evidence turned up. Gibson, on his own at his home, decided to go through a bag of garbage and remnants taken from a burn barrel seized by the FBI during the course of their investigation from Trudo's home. In going through the rubbish, Gibson saw a piece of brown paper not more than one inch square, a piece of paper that the FBI investigators had missed. It turned out this small piece of paper was part of a money wrapper and it had the Merchants Bank date stamp on it. As my client's house was some twenty-five miles from the scene of the robbery and was off a remote town road at the end of a long driveway, it was hard to suggest that the wrapper had simply floated up to my client's residence.

This was the first time I had represented a defendant in a federal court proceeding where multiple defendants with their respective counsel were being tried together before a single jury. I would finish a cross-examination and leave it right where I wanted it, only to be followed by Doug Pierson who tiptoed through his cross-examination without disrupting too much of what had already been accomplished. Both of us were followed by Bill Knight who plowed through the same ground, but with a heavy foot undoing much of what Doug and I thought we had gained through our previous cross-examinations.

At trial a witness identified the defendants as passengers in a car near the bank shortly before the robbery. She indicated she thought the driver might have been Roy Girard, but she couldn't say for sure. On cross examination, I asked her how she had made the identification. She said that she had been shown a book of pictures of possible suspects and recognized the defendants. She added that Roy Girard's picture looked most like the person that she had seen driving the car but couldn't swear to it. I asked for the book of pictures and the government gave it to me. I started to review it to myself, standing in front of the jury. I became fascinated, as it was not until the eleventh page before there was a picture of someone I had not previously represented.

The highlight of the trial, however, was when Roy Girard was called to the stand. He was in custody on another charge and had been moved that day to the sixth floor holding cell of the federal courthouse. The government called Roy as their next witness, and the judge directed the U.S. marshals to bring Mr. Girard to the courtroom.

One should have in mind how the courtroom looked at this

point. The judge was sitting at the head of the courtroom on an elevated bench. On a level just below him and in front of the bench was the court clerk, and at the next level sat the court reporter. On the right side of the courtroom facing the jury box was a table for the judge's law clerk, and then, facing the bench, three tables for the defendants and their attorneys. The prosecutors' table was closest to the jury, also facing the bench. There were fourteen jurors, a twelve-person jury plus two alternates, seated in the jury box, on the left side of the courtroom. There were numerous spectators and representatives of the press sitting at the back of the courtroom. I was sitting next to my client directly in the middle of the courtroom facing the bench with the co-defendants and their attorneys to my right. The courtroom was on the fifth floor of the courthouse, and to the immediate right of the bench there was a door leading down from the holding cell on the sixth floor. Ordinarily, this door was used for access to the courtroom when the defendant was in custody. In our case, however, all defendants were out on bail and the only person being held, albeit on a different charge, was Roy Girard.

There was a long pause and then a commotion in the hallway leading down to the door entering into the courtroom. The door burst open and out came Roy Girard and four U.S. marshals, one holding onto each of his legs and one holding each of his arms. He was squirming and fighting them all the way. The attention of everyone in the courtroom was riveted on Girard as he was carried across the entire courtroom towards the witness chair, located between the bench and the jury. He was paying little attention to the courtroom proceedings until he got halfway across the room. He looked up and saw me, and recognizing me, he immediately gave a smile and a short friendly wave. He then returned to his struggle with the marshals. Such a scene was not at all what I would have wished for.

He was placed in the witness chair by the four marshals who stayed nearby. He was asked to take the oath and he did not comply. He was asked to give his name and he refused. Finally, the judge, with a sense of frustration, turned to the marshal and said, "Get him out of here." This time they did not have to carry him. He leaped from the witness chair and started walking back across the courtroom towards the stairway up to his cell. As he approached the doorway, he turned to the defendants and gave them all the thumbs up sign. A big help.

All defendants have a right but no duty to testify in their own behalf. In this case the defendants decided not to take the stand. Finally the time came for closing argument. The government had the weakest case against George Tatro, the person who was supposed to be the friendly gun holder. The structure of my closing was basically that there was no evidence to hold George Tatro in this case, other than that he had been at a poker game with some unexplained one hundred dollar bills in his possession; obviously, that was not enough evidence to convict him, and if you cannot convict him, you should not convict my client, Calvin Trudo.

The case was submitted to the jury on Friday and they failed to reach a verdict by Friday night. They were sent home and told to return Saturday morning. The deliberations continued on Saturday morning and then well on into the afternoon before we were notified that the jury had reached a verdict. We were all back in the court-room, defense counsel and the defendants at their respective tables, Cook and Gibson at theirs. The jury filed back in and we all rose as the judge took the bench.

The jury announced their verdict of guilty as to all three defen-dants. After being thanked by the judge for their service, the jurors went back to the jury room to gather their belongings. The court continued the bail on the defendants pending sentencing, and we, at this point, all walked out of the courtroom. I was on my way down the hall when one of the jurors, having retrieved his coat, was coming down the same hallway. He called, "Oh, Mr. Langrock." I responded, "Yes?" He said, "I just wanted to let you know I thought you tried a hell of a good case. If I was ever in trouble and needed a lawyer, I'd hire you. Too bad your client was guilty." A lesson learned. Trudo was sentenced to serve eighteen years, and the Tatro brothers each to serve fifteen years. Eventually their convictions were affirmed by the U.S. Court of Appeals.[2]

That is not the end of the story. George Tatro, after the verdict and while out on bail pending his appeal on the bank robbery charge, was arrested for trying to rob a Vermont state liquor store. He was apprehended and convicted in a state court and sentenced to the state correctional system. Because the state sentence took effect first, he was under the control of the state system. He was a model prisoner, with no previous record, and so it was not long before he was walking the streets on a furlough. This meant he was still technically in state custody but was not kept in jail. One day I received a call from none other than George Tatro. The conversation went like this: "Peter, this is George Tatro." I said, "How are you, George?" He said, "I'm doing fine. I've gotten married, I'm working hard, I'm on furlough, and I'm doing well within the correctional system." I said, "That's fine." He said, "Peter, I just wanted to say one thing. I remember our trial in the bank robbery case and I remember how hard you argued for me, and I really appreciated that." (He apparently failed to appreciate that I wasn't so much arguing for him as trying to tie my client to the apron strings of the government's weakest case.) He continued, "I really do appreciate it and I would like to invite you and your wife out for dinner sometime just to say thank you." I said, "George, I don't think I've got time for that, but, maybe, in a few months we could do lunch."

4.
LAWERS, CLIENTS, & QUIRKS

Sometimes practicing law would be easier without clients. On one occasion Middlebury attorney Jack Conley wished at least that his client wasn't present. Jack came up to Burlington to the Chittenden Superior Court to defend Joe "The Barber" Cabrera on a charge of kidnaping. Merle Wood was the owner of the Country Store, Inc. in Winooski. In the early 1960s, this was Vermont's first and only major discount store. Merle had both a lady friend, Ruth Clark, and a lot of money. Cabrera was charged, among others, with kidnaping Ms. Clark in the hope of obtaining a tidy ransom from Mr. Wood.

Jack thought he had a decent defense, as the identification of his client was in some doubt. The kidnappers had pulled nylon stockings over their face, making a visual identification nearly impossible. The trial began, and the state called Ms. Clark to the stand. In response to the question, "How can you identify the defendant if he had a nylon stocking over his face?" She responded, "Well, I recognize him, as one time he lifted the stocking up off of his face." As she finished that statement, Cabrera turned to Conley and, in a whisper just loud

34

enough for the jury to hear, said, "The lying bitch, I never pulled that stocking up."

It didn't take long for the jury to convict.

Justice Albert Barney, in writing the opinion for the supreme Court, affirming the conviction, started by saying, "The respondent was convicted as a principal in the magnificently inept criminal episode . . . ."[3]

Arraignment day at the Chittenden District Court is a zoo. There are always dozens of citizens appearing for arraignment on a variety of charges ranging from one of "minor in possession of malt beverage" to serious felonies. Some of these people are represented by private attorneys, some by public defenders, and some by nobody but themselves. On one arraignment day when Judge Edward Costello was sitting on his elevated bench in the old Chittenden District courtroom, I arrived late to represent a client charged with DWI. By the time I got to court, everything was in full swing, and all I could do was take a seat in the back of the courtroom and wait my turn. Ordinarily, the judge would take the arraignments of those represented by private counsel first. I was too late for that special privilege.

I had clipped out a cartoon from a magazine which depicted a person driving a car that had been stopped by a police officer. The cartoonist made it clear that the person driving the car had been drinking. The caption read, "But officer, I was just hurrying home before the alcohol took effect." I took this cartoon, put it in an envelope, addressed the envelope to Judge Costello, and gave it to the bailiff who was overseeing the court proceedings. The bailiff walked up the steps to the back of the bench and handed the envelope to Judge Costello. Without pausing in the proceeding, Judge Costello proceeded to open the envelope, and with a slight smile, but without interrupting the lawyer who was then addressing the court, wrote a note on the cartoon, put it back in the envelope, and handed it back to the bailiff with instructions to return it to me. When the bailiff handed me the envelope, I took the cartoon out and there was Judge Costello's notation, "What was your client's test?" This didn't help my client get pushed to the top of the list for arraignment nor did it help in the eventual disposition of that case. What it was typical of, though, is the level of congeniality and the relaxed sense of atmosphere that existed between the bench and the bar in Judge Costello's courtroom. Unfortunately, with the advent of metal detectors at the entrance of the courthouse, and where attorneys as officers of the court have their pocket knives taken away from them as potential weapons, and where the judge's chambers are now separated from the masses and the bar in general by locked doors, this type of tomfoolery and lightheartedness has been substantially dissipated.

Allan Bruce is an institution as a lawyer in the City of Burlington. Not only is he a good lawyer, but he has been around long enough to have been involved in almost every type of case. His most endearing quality, however, is an absolutely great wit and a wonderful sense of humor. Judge Costello, who reigned over the Chittenden District Court from its creation in 1963 during Phil Hoff's first term as governor, loved lawyers and especially those who practiced in front of him. A sense of humor was never wasted on this judge, and Allen Bruce was one of his favorite lawyers.

In one notable case, Allan Bruce was representing a gentlemen who was charged with driving while under the influence of alcohol. The case was being prosecuted by State's Attorney Patrick Leahy. Allan used every argument he could in dealing with the state's attorney to try to get the charge reduced from a DWI charge to a lesser offense. He had no luck. Leahy knew he had a sound case and insisted upon a plea of guilty to the original charge. The time came when Allan had to fish or cut bait, and his client finally decided that he would plead guilty to the charge rather than go to a jury trial that he was almost sure to lose.

The big courtroom on the second floor of the old Chittenden District Court on Pearl Street was large, but dimly lit. There were risers to the bench and counsel stood at a podium at the base looking up at the judge. The bench was much higher from the floor than in most courtrooms and resembled a throne; a fitting position for Judge Edward "The Only" Costello. On this particular occasion, Allan Bruce and his client approached the podium and indicated that there was gong to be a plea of guilty. The judge went through the usual script, the plea was entered, the state's attorney made his recommendation, and a fine was imposed. Ordinarily, that would have closed the matter completely. But Allan rose and turned to the bench saying, "Your Honor, I would just like to make one additional statement." The court gave him permission. Allan started, "Your Honor, I just want you to know that if I ever need a heart transplant," and then with a pause and a nod over towards the state's attorney, he continued, "I hope I can have the state's attorney's, because it's never been used."

One day in the mid-1970s, I received a call from a young man who wanted me to represent him in connection with a charge that he possessed three pounds of marijuana. The authorities were charging him with the felony of possession of marijuana with intent to distribute. Apparently, they felt that three pounds was a bit more than he needed for purposes of personal consumption. I talked to him briefly and we set up a follow-up appointment. He said that his uncle, Al, sometimes known as "Big Al," would be coming with him. I was sitting in my office, and just before the appointed hour, I happened to look out my window to see a very large bright yellow Cadillac convertible with Florida plates pull up in front of the office. Out of the car appeared my client, and presumably "Big Al."

Shortly thereafter, they were ushered into my office, and my client introduced me to his uncle. After a few pleasantries, "Big Al" turned to me and said, "How much is it going to cost for you to represent my nephew?"

I told him, as this was a felony and a serious matter, I would require a retainer of twenty-five hundred dollars. He responded, "I don't want to talk about a retainer, I want to know how much it's going to cost me to have you represent him." I said that it is difficult to estimate how much time it would take when we don't know whether there will be a trial, but added I would be willing to take on the case through trial for a fixed fee of thirty-five hundred dollars. He then asked, "Well, what if there's an appeal?" I said if he wanted me to put a flat fee on everything in the case, including the possibility of an appeal, I would charge a flat fee of five thousand dollars. He then said, "Well, you'd have some expenses on top of that, wouldn't you?" I said, "Yes," paused and continued "Six thousand dollars should cover all the work I would have to do in the case and any expenses."

To this he responded, "Okay, I'll give you seven thousand dollars to cover everything." He then added, "And now, how much for the judges?"

I was a bit taken aback and I told him that we didn't do things that way in Vermont. He said, "What do you mean? I've been all over the country. There's always a way to get to the judges." I told him that Vermont was not all over the country and that his approach was completely out of line.

He backed off and said, "Okay," and gave me a retainer of twenty-five-hundred dollars. After a considerable amount of effort, we were finally able to arrive at a negotiated plea, where my client would avoid going to jail. My total bill fell between the twenty-five-hundred-dollar figure he had paid and the seven thousand dollars he had offered. I never got another nickel.

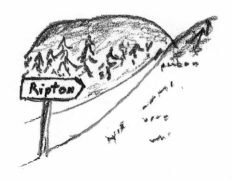

5.

MOUNTAIN MEN FROM RIPTON

George Farr, who served Addison County as deputy sheriff, as municipal judge and as county court clerk, was a true Vermont character in his own right. He is not to be confused with two other men who lived in Ripton and who also carried the name George Farr. George Farr, Sr. lived in a house on the North Branch Road in Ripton, Vermont. He was a volatile man, well-known for his quick temper. In the 1950s and 60s he made a living by buying and selling timber, trading woodlots, and pulling off the odd deal.

Ripton, a mountain town east of Middlebury, is the home of the Breadloaf Campus of Middlebury College, as well as the adopted home of America's poet laureate, Robert Frost. In the nineteenth century it was a thriving community and by 1870 had many small farms, seven sawmills and a population of six hundred and nineteen. As Vermont moved from the nineteenth century into the twentieth century, many of Ripton's hill farms were abandoned and the land was allowed to grow back to second growth timber. Its population had declined to two hundred and seven by 1960. During the depression of the 1930s, the United States government put together the Green

Mountain National Forest and purchased large tracts of land in Ripton as part of that forest. The title work that was necessary for the federal government's acquisition of lands helped keep some local lawyers from going broke during hard times. The national forest now comprises over two-thirds of all the lands in the town, and each year Ripton gets a payment from the federal government in lieu of taxes as a result of the sale of logs to private logging contractors.

Despite the large amount of land owned by the national forest, there are still numerous private woodlots that are owned by either logging companies or individuals. George Farr, Sr. was one of those individuals who owned woodlots.

The federal government had carefully surveyed the lands that it acquired and placed appropriate survey markers at various points as designated on their surveys. On occasion, those survey markers would come up missing or appear to have been moved. On more than one occasion, federal forest rangers, while walking on lands they believed belonged to the United States Government, were confronted by George Farr, Sr. and told to get the hell off his property. To back up his claim, he would point to the survey markers, indicating that the land was part of an adjacent lot that he owned, and not part of the Green Mountain National Forest. Whether or not the markers had been moved or who moved them became fodder for lawsuits. The federal government accused George Farr, Sr. of stretching his boundaries, and he told them to mind their damned business and stay the hell off his land. Because of his reputation for a bad temper, there eventually came an order out of the National Forest regional office that nobody was to go on lands claimed by or adjacent to lands owned by George Farr, Sr. without an armed U.S. marshal with them. Fortunately, despite the intimidating temper of George Farr, Sr., nothing more than a yelling match ever occurred, and finally titles were compromised and straightened out in court.

George Farr, Sr. had two sons. David left the confines of Ripton at an early age to join a carnival. He was a successful carny, and would return each year after his trips around the country with cash in hand, driving a Corvette. His brother, George, Jr., decided to stay in Ripton and follow in his father's footsteps.

Ripton was a good example of a real Vermont mountain town where, during the 1930s, 40s, and 50s, there was not much love for either the federal or the state government. It had its own code of law.

As a part of the Ripton tradition carried on from the days of prohibition, alcohol was not an unknown stranger. Danny Dragon, who had a farm on the road leading from the North Branch Road up to Abby Pond, and who once traded a large wooded area at the north end of Lake Dunmore for a team of horses, had a still built right into his house, with the telltale smoke from the still coming out through the chimney. George Farr, Jr. was known to support this tradition.

Up in the hills the north branch of the Middlebury River follows the dirt road known simply as the North Branch Road. Where that road joins the Lincoln-Ripton Road, a mountain road connecting the towns of Lincoln and Ripton, there was a tar paper shack inhabited by another of Ripton's characters, Peewee Brown. Peewee, according to locals, wasn't "all there." He survived by doing odd jobs, mainly for the smattering of down–country people who had purchased old farms as second homes in the Ripton area. One of those who hired Peewee Brown was a part-time Riptonite, William Hazlitt Upson, the author of the Earthworm tractor stories that were so popular in *The Saturday Evening Post*.

Peewee seemed to have enough money to keep himself in food, pay the minuscule amount of taxes on his tar paper shack, and even pay his electric utility bill, which was rather small, as he had only a single unshaded bulb hanging down from the ceiling on a wire in the middle of his home.

One warm summer night in 1974 George Farr, Jr. and a friend of his, a neighbor to Peewee, decided to party. Well into their second six-pack, they decided they would try out some newly acquired rifles. What better way could they test these new rifles than to fire tracer shells into the air. Peewee, hearing the shots and seeing the tracers fired into the air, stepped out of his shack, and with proper Ripton obscenities, voiced an objection to their activities. This triggered a decision by Farr and friend to use the single light bulb that was visible through the single window in Peewee's shack as a target. They were doing their drinking and shooting from the front yard of the friend's house, which was well within rifle range of Peewee's home. Peewee did not take kindly to their new venture, and after shouting a few more epithets, loaded his double-barreled twelve-gauge shotgun and his twenty-two caliber pistol. He put his pistol in his belt, grabbed the shotgun, and headed for the residence where George and his buddy were engaging in this rather unusual target practice.

Peewee was not subtle in his approach. He came at George Farr, Jr., pointing his twelve-gauge right at him. Somehow George managed to get hold of the end of the barrel and both shots discharged into the air. Breathing a quick sigh of relief, George failed to notice Peewee pulling the pistol from his belt. Peewee promptly fired a single shot from it into Farr's gut. Farr said, "Peewee, you son-of-a-bitch, you shot me." That apparently was sufficient satisfaction for Peewee to return to his home. Peewee's single light was still burning, although his window had been thoroughly smashed by the gun fire. During the ruckus with the shotgun, George's friend decided that the better part of valor was to get the hell out of there. This left George Farr, Jr. to himself with a bullet wound through his abdomen, no telephone, some six or seven miles from the nearest hospital, and about a half a mile to the closest neighbor. George, in the true tradition of a Riptonite, didn't think too much of the situation and promptly got in his car and drove ten miles to Porter Hospital in Middlebury. Although the bullet had done substantial damage it had avoided all the major organs, and after some surgery and a hospital stay, he fully recovered.

The state was then faced with the question of whether any or at least what criminal charges should be brought against the participants in this Ripton shootout. The Attorney General's Office was called in and Assistant Attorney General William Keefe, after talking to Upson and other Ripton residents, decided that the real instigator of this offense had been George Farr, Jr. The only charges brought were against Farr for reckless use of the rifle. While there was no law on the books which would give Peewee the right to avenge the use of his light bulb as a target by first trying to kill George Farr, Jr. with a shotgun, and then by firing a pistol pointblank into his stomach, it was decided that given Peewee's mental abilities, the overall justice of the situation dictated that no criminal charges would be brought against him.

A few months later the matter was finally resolved. The charges against Farr were reduced to the breach of the peace and Farr paid a twenty-five dollar fine. Such was the allocation of justice coming out of Ripton in the 1970s.

Bucky Dragon was from Ripton, a mountain man in every sense of the word. He was rugged, good looking, and tough. He had his own sense of values which did not always coincide with society's. Over the years, he got involved in a lot of different legal hassles and developed dual reputations throughout Addison County, first as a nemesis to law enforcement officers, and second as a folk hero to those people who sometimes found themselves living near the edge of the law.

While Bucky was not concerned with the liquor laws, driving laws, or the fish and game laws, he was insistent upon the fact that his word was his bond. I often represented Bucky. In one case I found myself on the other side. My client claimed that Bucky had crossed the boundaries of the property he was logging and had taken several nice logs on my client's side of the property line. The client was worried about taking on Bucky, thinking of possible reprisal. We settled this case fairly and my client never had any further problems. In all the time I represented Bucky or dealt with him, I had never known him to go back on his word to me.

Bucky was sentenced to the house of correction in Windsor to do hard time when he was only sixteen years old. This was as the result of his participation in a burglary at what used to be Beckwith Motors. His codefendants got off nearly scot-free, and this left a chip on Bucky's shoulder where law enforcement was concerned. Over the years he was in and out of jail on numerous occasions. When he was out of jail, he was a hard worker and a hard player. When he was in jail, he assumed a leadership role and was respected as someone to look up to by the other inmates. He was big enough and strong enough that he was able to maintain this leadership position from a physical as well as a "smarts" position.

In the early 1970s, Bucky was at the Windsor State Prison when a riot occurred. The prisoners had taken control of a cell block and were holding four hostages, burning mattresses, and tearing sinks from the cells and dropping them from the third tier of cells. They started making demands on the Department of Corrections.

Cornelius Hogan, who is at the time of this writing is secretary of human services for the state of Vermont, was then the deputy commissioner of corrections. On this particular occasion, Commissioner Kent Stoneman was out of town and it was up to Hogan to deal with the riot. He had gotten a call from the warden at the prison, Robert Smith, who told him, "They have four of my men as hostages — I'm going in with gas." Hogan said, "Hold the gas," and then set a speed record getting from his home in Berlin to Windsor.

When he got to Windsor, things were still chaotic, but the prisoners had indicated a willingness to negotiate and had released two hostages as a gesture of good faith. Hogan and Smith agreed to meet with a negotiating team of prisoners. The negotiating team consisted of Bucky, Bernard Woodmansee and Larry Ellerson. The Windsor prison had been built in 1807 (Thomas Jefferson was president), and although the three–tier cell blocks were newer, it would have made a great location for a 1930s movie set in a high security state pen. The captain's room was located next to the main control room, and was adjacent to the cell block where the riot was occurring. It was chosen as the site for the negotiations. A table was set up in the center of the ten–by–twenty–foot room with two chairs on one side and three chairs on the cell block side. There was a small lavatory located to the right of the prisoners' chairs. As Hogan and Smith took their seats, a fully armed state trooper burst out of the lavatory. The warden jumped up and pushed him back in, slamming the door shut, just as the inmates' negotiation team arrived. One of the agreed ground rules was that the State Police not be part of the direct negotiations. His presence could have blown the whole thing.

As the inmates entered the room, Hogan's jaw dropped. They were stark naked. The Warden leaned over to Hogan and said, "This is the way we negotiate with prisoners at Windsor."

AN ASIDE

In 1966 I represented a sixteen-year-old, Ronald Rich, who, as a disciplinary measure, was stripped naked and placed in a holding cell next to the old electric chair, only to be discovered in this condition by some members of the state Legislature touring the prison. This incident resulted in litigation[4] and eventually some reforms in the correction system. Nakedness, however, was still in vogue at the State prison in the 1970s.

The three inmates sat down in their chairs and discussions began. Their demands called for an orderly process for getting back to normal, but they wanted to be assured of no retribution or prosecution for what had already occurred.

Ellerson, sporting a long and bushy Fu Manchu moustache, which he would pull down on with both hands as if he were milking a cow, was agitated and clearly on the edge. He had spent almost as much time in the criminal mental wards at the Vermont State Hospital as he had at the state prison.

Woodmansee, a very bright, and in a perverse way, perhaps brilliant individual, seemed to appreciate and enjoy the key role he was playing in the history of the prison and did most of the talking.

Dragon was quiet and spoke only at key moments in the negotiations. He was the one who seemed to make sense. He apparently realized there could be no good outcome from what was happening and was looking for a solution where everybody could save some face and no one would get hurt.

After about an hour, the talks came to an end with some fundamental agreement as to what would and would not happen next. Everyone stood up and shook hands. As Bucky was shaking hands with Hogan, he said, "Don't worry, it will happen."

After the inmates left, Hogan turned to Smith and asked if he believed the inmates would deliver on their end of the negotiations. Smith responded that he believed they would: "Bucky Dragon is a man of his word." He was right, and in short time the prison returned to its normal routine.

Another son of Ripton, albeit an adopted one, is Foster "Mac" McEdward. Mac is a pilot. He was born in Maine in 1921 and now spends much of his time at Eagles' Nest in Ripton, a home he has built high up on a rocky crag surrounded by the Green Mountain National Forest. Foster is often seen driving through Middlebury in his bright red pickup decked out with a dozen American flags flying in the breeze and an Old Town canoe strapped to the top.

In 1960, just back from a flying stint in Saudi Arabia, he was at Gefion Fountain in Copenhagen when he spotted a beautiful young blonde Danish woman, Kirsten, and fell instantly in love. Fortunately for Mac, Kirsten fell in love with him as well. Shortly thereafter he and his new bride were off on a flying job in Egypt.

As a young man in World War II, Mac had flown the hump in Burma for General Chennault and his Flying Tigers. After leaving the air force, he continued his aviation career doing a variety of things, including flying mapping missions for private companies that were funded by the CIA. Kristin gave birth to two beautiful blonde daughters, Jackie and the younger, Penny, who was the same age as my oldest son. As families, we became good friends. In 1964, Foster asked me if I would be interested in going to Afghanistan with him as his ground man on a contract he had been offered by what was most assuredly a CIA–funded company, to use modern photographic equipment for a mapping of Afghanistan. My job would have been to make sure there were representatives of Russia, Afghanistan, and the United States on each plane to assure no untoward accidents happened. As interesting as the proposal was, I declined, and after some delays, Mac ended up in Afghanistan in 1965. Despite not being able to go with him, I was still his attorney. Over the years whenever he had a legal problem, whether it was a blown engine in New Mexico or an inspection problem in Alaska, I would get a call and be expected to give instant advice.

As time went on and Mac's family started to grow up, he curtailed his world jaunts and took a job as chief pilot for Air North, a small commuter airline which was based in Burlington. It was while flying a charter for Air North that Foster met John C. Lobb, who was the new CEO of Northern Electric Co., a major Canadian corporation which manufactured and supplied virtually all of the telephone equipment for Canada. The company was perceived as having grown fat from its relatively unchallenged share of the market and Lobb was brought in as a hatchet man to trim that fat. Mac did not know much about Lobb, but as he flew some special charters for him as an Air North pilot, he got to like him. On one of these flights Lobb, who had learned to respect Foster's flying abilities, especially his total commitment to safety, asked him if he would be interested in coming to Montreal to run Northern Electric's new internal aviation program. When he added that Northern Electric was obtaining some new Grumman Gulfstreams for its domestic flights for its own executives, Mac became even more interested. He inquired about salary, benefits, and security, and Lobb told him that they would have a gentlemen's agreement that the job would last for two or three years, at a minimum, and offered him an attractive salary and benefit package.

Mac and Lobb shook hands on the deal right there on the airplane. Shortly thereafter, Mac gave Air North notice, and in December of 1973 he started his new career as head of a corporate aviation department.

Unfortunately, after about six months Lobb reversed his policy about the expansion of an internal corporate aviation department and started wielding his hatchet. Foster was the first to go. Mac found himself an unemployed pilot at the age of fifty-three and with no immediate place to go. He came to see me, and we brought suit against Northern Electric. Doug Pierson, a Burlington lawyer, was retained by Northern Electric to defend the case.

It was a difficult one for us, as we had no written contract. Our only evidence was Mac's recollection of the conversation that took place on the airplane to the effect that there was a gentlemen's agreement that the job would last a minimum of two or three years. It was important for our case to get Lobb's recollection of what was said on that airplane ride. As the CEO of a major corporation, he felt he had better things to do than to be deposed in a simple contract dispute. Eventually, however, we were able to obtain a date when he would be available for a short deposition in Montreal. I drove to Montreal and we met up with Lobb, a group of his staff members, and Doug Pierson at an office near Dorval Airport. While waiting to start the deposition, Lobb's staff appeared to be totally intimidated by him, and it was quite clear he was not happy about having his deposition taken.

When we finally got started, I asked a series of general questions about the company, its plans for an internal aviation department, and Foster's responsibilities in that regard. This was before getting to the crux of the matter, the conversation that took place on the airplane concerning the handshake and the making of a gentlemen's agreement.

When finally questioned about the specific conversations that evening in the airplane, Lobb claimed to have little memory of what had transpired. I asked him if he recalled whether he had a conversation with Mr. McEdward and had promised him by way of a gentlemen's agreement a two or three–year contract with Northern Electric. He said that he never made any such agreement. The next question: "What would you say if Foster McEdward said that the two of you shook hands after you had said, 'We'll have a gentlemen's agreement of a two or three-year contract'?" Lobb responded, "Foster McEdward would be an unmitigated liar." I asked one further question, "Would you be willing to come to Vermont and testify to that at the trial?" He said, "Yes." That ended the deposition.

The case came to trial in the federal court building in Rutland, Vermont, before Judge James Holden, a former military officer himself, who had served as chief justice of the Vermont Supreme Court before being appointed to the more lucrative federal judgeship. The courtroom was located on the second floor of the courthouse located on West Street. It is a beautiful courtroom and, unlike most others, instead of the usual dark paneled wood walls, the motif of the courtroom is white Vermont marble and blue cloth paneling.

The trial was relatively short. Mac took the stand and told his story. He told about his service in World War II and flying the Burma Hump for Chennault as a member of the Flying Tigers. He continued with his experiences flying in Saudi Arabia, Egypt, Afghanistan, and most of the rest of the world. He then told the story of how he met John Lobb and of their conversations on the plane. His appearance on the stand with his closely cropped haircut, immaculately neat clothing, and military bearing, made a favorable impression on the jury. Lobb never showed up, and as his deposition was read into evidence, the jury paid close attention. The jury had a choice to make. They could either believe Lobb, who had failed to show up as promised and had referred to Foster McEdward as an "unmitigated liar," or they could believe Mac. Mac may have had some weaknesses in his case, but no one who saw him testify would ever characterize him as an "unmitigated liar."

The time came for the judge to charge the jury and decide whether or not in fact he would even let the case go to the jury. It was a close question, as we had no written contract, and even our alleged oral contract was somewhat ambiguous as to its terms. Fortunately, in researching the case law for the trial, I had found an old Alaska territorial case involving a bush pilot who was terminated under similar circumstances and where the federal territorial court allowed the plaintiff to prevail. Based upon that case, Judge Holden submitted our case to the jury. The jury was not out long before they brought back a verdict for every penny we asked, including interest.

Even more important than the money judgment granted in favor of Mac was his belief that he had been vindicated. It seemed as the jury came back and announced the verdict, Foster regained almost instantaneously all of the confidence and pride he had previously had as a pilot flying all over the globe.

AN ASIDE

While the case was pending, Mac found himself a job as chief pilot for International Shoe Machinery Company, where he flew DC-4s around the world containing displays of equipment manufactured by the company.

Not surprisingly, Northern Electric took an appeal from the judgment to the Second Circuit Court of Appeals. My former partner, and now judge of that same Court of Appeals, Fred Parker, argued the case on behalf of McEdward. On the three-judge panel hearing the case were two Vermonters, Judge Sterry Waterman and Judge James Oakes, as well as Judge Charles Edward Wyzanski, an unusual character and a federal district judge in Massachusetts who was sitting as a visiting judge. More than one year after the argument and by a two-to-one vote, they ruled that there was not a sufficient showing concerning the contract to allow the judgment to stand. Thankfully, however, instead of reversing the case outright, they remanded it for a new trial.[5] Before proceeding to a second trial, we were able to settle the case.

The mountain men of Ripton include people who are there only for a few days a year for deer hunting, and, more important for some of them, the accompanying poker games. Two of us, Bill Rule and I, had bought from David Farr a small log cabin with a big stone fireplace on ten acres of land which we used as a deer hunting camp.

One deer season after the first day of hunting, we invited our neighbors from the camp about a half mile down an old logging road, to join our guest, Francis O'Brien, and us for a few beers and some cards. Francis was known as a bit of a card shark, having honed his skills at various commission sales while waiting for cattle auctions to begin. As the evening went on, even though we were playing for rather moderate stakes, Francis was doing quite well. He suggested a round of "in between," a game sometimes known as "acey-deucey" or "red dog." In that game each player puts up a modest ante and then is dealt two cards. The player to the left of the dealer has the first opportunity to place a bet, up to the amount of the pot, that the next card dealt will fall in between the two cards that have been dealt previously. If the card does fall within the two dealt cards, the player takes a sum matching the bet from the pot. If the card that is turned up is the same as one of the player's two cards or falls outside the two cards, then that player must place an amount equal to his bet in the pot. If the pot is not exhausted by the end of the first round, the dealer then deals out two new cards to each player. This time, the play starts with the person who is second to the left of the dealer. The game has the potential for growing a large pot very rapidly, as players often bet the entire pot only to find the cards less than kind, forcing them to match the pot. If this happens four or five times in a row, the pot can get quite large.

On this particular evening the cards were not kind to the players, and by the end of the fifth round, the pot was in excess of fifty dollars. On the sixth round, it was to be Francis' chance to bet first. He dealt the cards and it turned out that he had a deuce/king. The player immediately to his left who would have the second chance at the pot had an ace/deuce. Francis quite confidently said he was going to bet the pot. At this point our visitor from the neighboring camp, sitting to the left of Francis, pulled a .38 revolver out of his holster and laid it on the table. He looked Francis directly in the eye saying, "This time you're going to deal from the top of the deck."

I strongly suggested to Francis that he should only bet half the pot. He did collect one-half of the pot when the card from the top of the deck fell in between his deuce and king. The player at the left won the other half of the pot when the next card fell in between his deuce and ace. The pistol went back into the holster and the game came to an abrupt end. We didn't invite those neighbors back for a card game the following deer season.

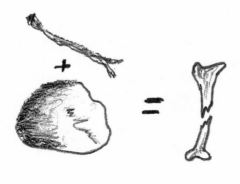

6.
STICKS & STONES

" Sticks and stones may break my bones, but names will never hurt me," the familiar childhood taunt, somehow loses its appeal as people grow older, and upon becoming adults people take name calling very seriously. We thus have the law of defamation, which includes libel, a written name calling, and slander, a verbal name calling.

Traditionally, it is often the newspapers that are accused of defaming some local citizen. Juries can get mad and express their anger in large verdicts when a newspaper carries false information about an individual. As damage to one's reputation is much harder to prove than the losses associated with a personal injury, such as a broken leg, the courts over time developed the concept of general damages, allowing a jury to award a sum they believe represents the harm done to the individual by the defamation, without the individual having to prove specific losses. For a long time an even further help to the defamed person was the principle of *per se* libel. This meant that if the statement fell into certain categories, such as an accusation of a crime, and that accusation was untrue, the jury would be told in effect that a libel had occurred and that they should award general damages.

All of this runs counter to the thrust of the First Amendment, which has as its main purpose the protection of free speech. The United States Supreme Court wrestled for many years with the conflict between the need to have a free and open dialog in our society and also a desire to protect individuals from untrue and often malicious stories printed about them. Justice Hugo Black maintained that all speech was protected and that there should be no law allowing recovery for defamation; other members of the court were more sympathetic to defamed citizens.

In 1964 the United States Supreme Court handed down a landmark decision in a case, *New York Times Co. v. Sullivan*. There they held that in cases involving public figures, even false statements were constitutionally protected unless they were made with malice. This set most of the previous state court legal decisions on their head and started all the courts on an evolutionary adventure to strike the proper balance between protecting an individual's good name and the need for a democratic society to have a free and open dialog.

Vermont's evolutionary adventure began on January 13, 1972, when a young woman was brought into the Central Vermont Hospital Emergency Room with a serious gunshot wound to her head. Paul Michelin was the emergency room doctor on duty. He recognized the seriousness of the wound, and after stabilizing the young woman, had her transported to the Medical Center Hospital in Burlington, which would give her more specialized care. Despite the advanced care she received, she died shortly after her arrival in Burlington.

The gunshot wound had been self-inflicted. Kenneth Roberts, a reporter for *The Times Argus* in Barre, had learned of the incident, and wanting to do a story, had contacted the Barre Police, the State Police, the sheriff's office, and the state's attorney's office, only to find that they had no knowledge of the incident. Vermont law required every physician treating a bullet wound to report the incident to local law enforcement officials "at once." It was a busy day in the emergency room and Dr. Michelin continued treating other patients, relying upon the staff to report the gunshot wound. After his shift was over, he was scheduled for a five-day vacation. Roberts, being aware of the responsibility of the physician to report the treatment of a gunshot wound, tried to reach Michelin. By the time he reached him, Roberts was frustrated and very aggressive in his conversations with the doctor. The doctor, a rather mild-mannered man, was taken aback by Roberts' accusation that he had committed a crime by not reporting the shooting. He was standing by his phone when he got the call and literally took a step back with the phone in his hand when the phone jack pulled out of the wall. Roberts thought Michelin had hung up on him and became even angrier.

The thrust of the articles that followed in *The Times Argus* was focused not upon the shooting itself, but upon Dr. Michelin's failure to report the shooting and the Vermont law that made it a crime for a doctor to fail to report a shooting. Dr. Michelin was relatively new to the Barre area. Roberts, in trying to get background information on the doctor, found some confusion among hospital officials as to Michelin's medical background and his staff status at the hospital. Besides focusing on and in effect accusing Dr. Michelin of having committed a crime, the articles also questioned the abilities of Dr. Michelin. Michelin was mad.

Paul came in to see me and requested that I bring a defamation action on his behalf. I told him I would consider doing so, but I suggested a sixty-day cooling off period to see how things worked out. During that period, Attorney General Kimberley Cheney investigated the matter and completely cleared Dr. Michelin. As usual, the newspaper, in reporting on the Attorney General's investigation, appeared more interested in justifying their previous two articles than they did in restoring Michelin's good name. At the end of the cooling off period, Paul came to see me and he was still mad. We brought suit.

There had been no cases in Vermont interpreting the evolving defamation law since the U.S. Supreme Court's 1964 decision in *Times v. Sullivan*. Thus, from a Vermont law standpoint we were charting some new ground at the trial level. The old law of Vermont had been modified by the U.S. Supreme Court decisions, and our job was to figure out the extent of those modifications, and to do so without any help from Vermont Supreme Court decisions.

The case was tried in the Washington County Courthouse in Montpelier. Charles "Chuck" Gibson defended Roberts and *The Times Argus*. In the course of negotiations he had offered one thousand dollars to settle the case. We demanded on Dr. Michelin's behalf the amount of seventy-five hundred dollars. Probably, five thousand dollars would have settled the case.

Newspapers generally follow the rule of "millions for defense, not a penny for tribute." For this reason, cases often go to trial because of the principles involved, rather than being settled on an amount that is fair, or, given the real costs of litigation, or what makes financial sense.

Judge Wynn Underwood was the trial judge in this matter, and after the evidence closed, we had long discussions in chambers about what law should be charged to the jury. Underwood stuck with the old law from the Vermont Supreme Court, as had been set out in an earlier case, *Lacoor v. Herald & Globe Association,* and charged the jury that in cases of libel *per se,* such as one where a person had been falsely charged with having committed a crime, malice could be presumed rather than proven. I argued with the judge that he was giving me a charge that was too favorable (a rather unusual occurrence), as the *Lacoor* case had been modified by the Supreme Court cases starting with *Times v. Sullivan.* He wouldn't back off from his charge and the case went to the jury in that fashion. After about two hours of deliberation, the jury came back and handed their verdict form to the court clerk who showed it to the judge, who then returned it to her to read it aloud in open court. You could see her counting the zeros before reading that the jury found in Michelin's behalf and awarded compensatory damages of thirty-five thousand dollars and punitive damages of seventy-five thousand dollars. This was a long way from the one thousand dollar offer that had been extended to us, and a long way from the seventy-five hundred dollars that we had indicated we would settle the case for.

As the verdict was read, you could feel both Michelin's excitement in having been vindicated and the shock and dismay of the defendants at the size of the verdict. As soon as the jury was dismissed, I met with my client in the plaintiffs' room in the front of the courthouse. I shut the door and reminded him that while we had won the verdict, it might not stand on appeal because of the judge's charge. He looked at me, and he said, "That may be true, but it sure is fun right now."

Virtually all plaintiffs' verdicts in cases against newspapers are appealed. This case was no exception. In his opinion, speaking for a unanimous supreme court, Justice Albert Barney held for Michelin in every way, except that he said the court was in error to charge the jury that they could presume malice in a *per se* libel case. The fact that the jury had to have found actual malice in order to award punitive damages was not enough to override the error in the charge, and the case was sent back for a new trial. We were able to settle the case before going to the second trial at a figure substantially higher than our previous demand, but admittedly lower than what the jury had awarded.

No one seems to value their good name and reputation more than lawyers themselves. John S. Burgess, who served Vermont as its lieutenant governor and was a long-time practicing lawyer in Brattleboro, Vermont, had a run in with the *Brattleboro Reformer*. In March, 1979, a grand jury was convened to investigate a possible embezzlement by the former president of the then-defunct Mark Hopkins College. There was never any question concerning John's integrity or any suggestion he was in any way involved in the missing funds. He had been a trustee and treasurer of the college, but it was clear that he had not been involved in any misappropriation. The *Brattleboro Reformer* ran a headline to an article that was for most part factually correct. It was the headline, "Grand Jury Probes Embezzlement, Burgess Denies Getting Funds" that angered Burgess. While literally true, it gave the impression to the casual reader that Burgess was somehow involved as a suspect in an embezzlement case. Judge Silvio Valente, sitting in the superior court in Windsor County, dismissed the action before trial on the grounds that because the headline was literally true, it was not libelous. Our office took an appeal to the Vermont Supreme Court. There were two questions of law: (1) Was Burgess a public figure for purposes of this case? (2) Could a headline under these circumstances form the basis for a defamation case? The Supreme Court held that although John had held several posts which would ordinarily qualify him as a public figure, he was not a public figure for all purposes and was not one in this case. The court also held that indeed a headline which was potentially as misleading as this should be submitted to a jury to determine whether or not it constituted defamation. They sent the case back for trial.

Ed Amidon, then my partner, and I went off to Newfane for a trial. Bob Erdmann, of Dinse, Erdmann & Clapp, defended the case for the *Reformer*. Once again, this was a case where the newspapers refused to discuss a settlement. No offer of settlement was ever made. After two days of trial and after several hours of deliberation, the jury reported that it was hopelessly deadlocked. A mistrial was declared.

Some months later, I came back to try the case a second time. One of the problems we had was that John's overall reputation was so high and he was so well known, that although he underwent real personal discomfort as a result of the article, it had done little, if anything, to damage his overall reputation. Again, the case was submitted to the jury, and again after several hours, they reported back that they were deadlocked. The judge sent them back to the jury room after giving additional instructions emphasizing how important it was that each of them reconsider their opinions to see if they could possibly return a verdict. About an hour later, they did in fact return a verdict, finding that the plaintiff had not proven his case of defamation.

John had had his day in court, and he felt good about at least having put the *Reformer* to the test as to what everybody agreed was an unfair headline.

Dan Ryan was accused in a series of articles in *The Rutland Herald* as being a truck driver who illegally hauled and dumped hazardous waste. The truth of the matter was that it was his cousin, Jack Ryan, who was deserving of the accusation. Once again, we were before Judge Silvio Valente, but this time in the Rutland Superior Court. Judge Valente overruled the defendant's motion to dismiss and the case was set for trial. Bob Hemley, a top trial attorney from Burlington, defended the *Herald*. We thought we had a pretty good case, as the reporter for the *Herald* was grossly negligent in not following through to see which Ryan was the illegal dumper. Dan testified that while he could show no direct loss of business, when he went to the stock car races he was kidded unmercifully about being the evil dumper. The case was submitted to the jury, and they returned a verdict of one dollar in actual damages, but expressed their outrage at the newspaper by bringing in a punitive damage award of five thousand dollars. As usual, the newspaper took an appeal. In his opinion, Justice Morse, writing for a unanimous Vermont Supreme Court, held that the facts of the case involving the gross negligence of the reporter did not rise to the constitutional requirement of actual malice and, therefore, could not support the punitive damage award. The court, however, felt there had been sufficient facts under the current state of the law to allow the one dollar actual damage award to stand. A Pyrrhic victory. I insisted that Bob Hemley send me a check for the one dollar, which I dutifully accounted to my client, with sixty-seven cents to him and thirty-three cents to our firm.

Many people come into our office feeling wronged by the press, inquiring whether they can bring suit. I always tell them I will consider the possibility of bringing suit, but not until after sixty days has passed. Almost always after sixty days people realize the damage inflicted by the false statement is not as great as they had imagined, and that the bringing of a lawsuit might only serve to emphasize the situation rather than solve any problem. There was one case that was an exception to this rule. Frank Kelly was a long-time teacher at Middlebury Union High School, finally serving as the school's principal. He retired and took an administrative post at Middlebury College. One day Frank arrived at work, only to be stopped by his good friend Jim Ross, who inquired, "Frank, are you in trouble?" Frank asked, "What do you mean?" Jim said he had heard on the radio that Frank was being charged with the sexual molestation of a high school student. Frank said, "Are you crazy?" Jim said he had heard it coming to work that morning. Frank promptly got hold of the local newspapers and listened to the radio to find, sure enough, they were reporting that Frank Kelly, former principal of Middlebury Union High School, was being charged with the sexual molestation of a high school student.

Frank was incensed, and within minutes he was at my office. A call to the State's Attorney's office informed us that another teacher with the same last name had indeed been charged, but that it had nothing whatsoever to do with Frank Kelly. We decided to bring suit immediately, not so much for the possibility of recovering an award, but to make the libel suit itself a news story that would be circulated and have the effect of informing all that the first story was obviously a mistake. The strategy worked, and within twenty-four hours everyone in the community was aware of the libel suit and that a mistake had been made by the newspapers and the local radio station. Frank Kelly continued to be held in the high esteem he always enjoyed in the community. This was one of a few times that the newspapers and radio station involved were willing to talk settlement. Frank, having accomplished his goal and not being interested in long, drawn out litigation, and realizing the matter had been a mistake rather than a malicious act, instructed me to seek a settlement. Within days that was accomplished and the case closed.

7.

BATTICK

On December 12, 1972 at 10:00 p.m., a shoot-out occurred at Whipple's Pharmacy on Route 7 in Manchester, Vermont. The Manchester Police were alerted to an alarm going off, indicating a burglary in progress. Upon arrival at the scene, Chief Dana L. Thompson and Officer George Hoag of the five-man Manchester Police Department entered the building looking for the perpetrators. As they moved into the store with guns drawn, they shouted a warning that whoever was in the building should come out with their hands up. Instead, unexpectedly, the police were met with gun shots. Chief Thompson was shot in the face at close range and died instantly. Officer Hoag was critically wounded in the abdomen by a .38 caliber bullet from the first volley of shots. Reinforcements were called for, and Officers James Webb and Eugene Gaotti responded. They began returning fire at the burglars.

Twenty-five year old Edward Battick and his twenty-four year old companion, Brian O'Keefe, had entered the drug store with the intention of stealing narcotics. Battick and O'Keefe, in the course of the gun fire, attempted to escape through a side door. They made it outside the building into the parking lot. Battick was then hit by the gun fire and he barricaded himself behind a car; O'Keefe made his escape as the gun fight continued. Eventually, Battick surrendered, sliding his revolver out from under the car toward the police. He was taken to the Putnam Memorial Hospital where it was determined that he had been shot seventeen times. The last four wounds occurred under circumstances which give rise to this story.

Despite the multiple gunshot wounds, Battick was still alive. After several days he was moved to the state's largest hospital in Burlington, where after several months of treatment, under guard at the hospital, he recovered. The cost to the taxpayers of medical expenses alone was eighty thousand dollars. The same medical services today would have a cost approaching a half million dollars.

Brian O'Keefe was captured after a twelve-hour manhunt in a remote camp on Lyons Brook Road outside of Manchester, where he surrendered without resistance.

Battick was subsequently charged with and convicted of first degree murder. His sentence was life imprisonment. In early December of 1975, just before the three year anniversary date of the shooting, Battick filed on his own a lawsuit in the federal court in Burlington, alleging that his civil rights had been violated. His legal papers complained that after he had surrendered in the shoot-out by throwing his gun out from under the car, Officer Eugene Gaotti of the Manchester Police Department had come over to where Battick was lying helpless on the ground, and fired four additional shots into his body. His complaint alleged that at the time Gaotti fired the shots, he had already received thirteen gunshot wounds, had been totally incapacitated, had surrendered, and was in no way a threat to Gaotti or anyone else. As unsympathetic a plaintiff as he was, it was clear that if he was right about what happened, his civil rights had been violated; even though Gaotti's chief had been killed and a fellow officer critically wounded, Gaotti would have had no right to deliberately shoot an unarmed Battick at point-blank range.

No attorney had agreed to represent Battick in connection with his civil case, and U.S. District Judge Albert Coffrin was faced with the prospect of having a jury trial in his court which would be conducted by Battick himself. The prospect of a person already convicted of first degree murder acting as his own lawyer in a civil rights claim against a police officer who was accused of shooting him was not at all appealing to the judge. If the facts as alleged by Battick were true, the case was an important one and should go forward, but Battick should be represented by a lawyer. Judge Coffrin asked me to take on the responsibilities of representing Battick, and I consented.

In July of 1977, the case came on for trial at the federal courthouse located on Pearl Street in Burlington. My associate, Susan Humphrey, agreed to assist me in the preparation and trial of the case. The Manchester Police Department had an insurance policy that protected their police officers in cases of a claim like this, and the insurance company retained James Haugh of Ryan Smith & Carbine of Rutland, perhaps the best insurance defense lawyer of the time, to represent Gaotti.

The case would be tried before a jury of six persons and two alternates. It was apparent that if Mr. Battick's claim was to succeed it would be necessary to get jurors who could look beyond the horrible acts admittedly committed by Battick, and reach an objective judgment on whether Gaotti had in fact fired the four shots in the manner claimed by Battick. Under these circumstances, Judge Coffrin gave the attorneys considerable leeway in their *voir dire,* in the hope of obtaining a jury that could be fair and objective under very difficult circumstances. My first question to the jury started with a statement: "If Vermont had capital punishment, I probably wouldn't be standing here today. My client would have undoubtedly been executed as a result of his commission of first degree murder in this case. If the State of Vermont no longer has the power to act as an executioner, even with all the protections the law allows, are you willing to judge the facts in this case, recognizing that no matter how horrendous the actions of Mr. Battick may have been, no individual may usurp authority and become a self-appointed executioner?" Many prospective jurors said they could not separate the actions of my client from the actions allegedly performed by Gaotti, and that they did not feel they could fairly sit on the case. After almost a full day of questioning the potential jurors, we were finally able to agree upon eight persons who indicated they could sit in the jury box and judge the actions of Gaotti, based on the facts as they were proven in court, without giving undue regard to the crime committed by my client.

Gaotti's defense was that he did not fire four shots at point blank range, and that all of the wounds received by Mr. Battick must have occurred during the gun fight. It was my job to prove to the jury what actually happened, and their job to render a fair verdict.

Battick was called to the stand and he testified that indeed he had fired the shots that had killed Chief Thompson and wounded Officer Hoag. He claimed that he had done so while he was under the influence of drugs during a burglary in which he was attempting to obtain narcotics to meet his body's cravings. He then detailed his recollection of the progress of the gun fight. He said he had finally hollered out, "It's all over," and had thrown his gun out from under the car he had been using as a barricade. He said the gun had fallen in full view of the officers. He then detailed how Officer Gaotti, coming from behind the building, had walked over to where he was lying, and while standing directly over him, had fired four shots into his body, the officer's gun being only a few feet from his chest.

In the course of the police investigation, it was discovered that an elderly woman by the name of Campisi, who was living in a house next to the pharmacy parking lot, had been attracted by the flashing lights and noises and had gone to her window. She testified that she had seen a man lying prone on the ground at the spot where Battick had been found, and that she saw another large man come around a corner of the building, walk over to him and stand above him, holding what appeared to be a pistol in his hand. She testified she heard four additional noises that sounded like shots, and that at each sound the right hand of the man standing over the prone figure had jerked upward.

During preparation of the case we discovered that Burlington attorney Saul Agel, who had been assigned to represent Battick in the criminal case, had retained a ballistics expert from Albany, Stanley Braverman. Braverman had made some tests on Battick's clothing, using photographic paper and a solvent. The tests showed a powder burn pattern indicating a gun had been fired at a distance of two to three feet from Battick. Jimmy Haugh challenged Braverman's qualifications and his methodology. The court ruled that there was a sufficient scientific basis to qualify him as an expert allowing him to render that opinion. The jury thus received as evidence Braverman's testimony that the shots had been fired within three feet of Battick's body.

In the defense, Haugh called several witnesses to the stand to describe the details of the shoot-out. Finally, Gaotti took the stand and testified that he did not fire the shots from a point blank range, and that any shots he had fired had come from a greater distance as he came around the building and before Battick had surrendered. The factual issues were clearly joined.

The time came for closing arguments, and I reiterated the position that while my client deserved no sympathy, he was clearly entitled as a matter of law to a damage award for the four shots he had received at the hands of Gaotti. Haugh argued that the police officer was under tremendous stress and that he should be believed when he said that any shots he fired occurred prior to Battick's surrender. He discounted Ms. Campisi's testimony, saying she was not in a good position to observe and was obviously confused. He further challenged Braverman's conclusions as unscientific, and belittled Battick's testimony as that of a convicted first degree murderer challenging the testimony of a police officer.

Judge Coffrin charged the jury on the law of the case, excused the alternates, and in mid-afternoon sent the jurors in to deliberate.

The toughest time for attorneys is waiting while the jury deliberates. At about six o'clock the judge inquired of the jury if they wished to continue deliberations and have some dinner brought in to them, or if they wished to adjourn for the day and come back on the following day. They indicated that they wished to continue with their deliberations and would like to have some food sent in to them. I remember well that one of the six jurors was a woman who ran a health food store and that the dinner order consisted of requests for five ham sandwiches and one apple.

Susan and I left the courthouse and had dinner. When we returned to the courthouse, the jury was deliberating and we went into the defendants' room to await the result of their deliberations. We had worked very closely on the case and our level of intensity was extraordinarily high. While waiting for the jury, we decided to play a game called Mastermind. Susan was to write down four numbers and I was to do the same, and then by asking various questions concerning the numbers, I was to try to figure out with a minimum of questions what numbers she had written on her piece of paper. She wrote down her four numbers, and I remember confidently writing down four numbers as well. They turned out to be the very same numbers she had chosen. Perhaps it was just the one in ten thousand chance that we came up with the same numbers; perhaps because of the intensity of the moment we had developed an ability to communicate in an unexplained way.

The evening wore on, and at regular intervals the judge inquired of the jury whether they wished to continue their deliberations that night or to come back the next day. Each time, they answered that they thought they were close to a verdict and would like to try to finish the case that night. Finally, at eleven thirty a marshal came and told us the jury had reached a verdict. We filed back into the courtroom. The foreperson of the jury gave the verdict form to the clerk, who handed it to the judge, who read it and then handed it back to the clerk to read to the assemblage for the official record. What she read were the jury's answers to the questions submitted by the court. The jury's finding was that Gaotti had violated Battick's civil rights. They awarded Battick five thousand dollars.

The jury had undertaken a terribly difficult task and, despite their aversion for Battick, had reached a verdict on what they believed to be the true facts. It was a tough case for the court, a tough case for Mr. Haugh, and a tough case for our office, but it was an even tougher case for the jurors, and their verdict was a triumph for the integrity of our jury system.

8.
SOME COURTHOUSES

One of the most picturesque courthouses in the entire world lies on the village green in Newfane, the shire town of Windham County. It sits back from Route 30, with a large green, a fountain, and impressive old maple trees leading up to its two story white columns setting off the front door. It was on that green, in front of the courthouse, that a case was settled involving some of Vermont's more interesting, if lesser known, characters.

Roger McBride was an attorney practicing in Windham County. He was also a politician, and in the early 60s a member of the conservative wing of the Republican party. I had met him at several political functions in 1960 and 1962 when I was running for state's attorney of Addison County. In the mid 60s, Roger decided that his political ambitions could be more realistically fulfilled in Washington, D.C., than in Vermont. He decided to close his practice and go to Washington to pursue some family interests in the TV series that was being made from the book, *A Little House on the Prairie*. In Washington he eventually headed the trucking industry's trade organization. Later he became the Libertarian Party's candidate for president of the United States.

When McBride left his practice, he asked me to complete three or four pieces of litigation in which he was counsel and which he would be unable to resolve before he left for the big city. One of these cases involved a libel action brought against George Trask, a realtor from the town of Winhall, and his firm, Trask & Waite. George was a good friend of Roger's, and they shared many political beliefs, the most important of which was to keep the government off the backs of the people. Trask later became the Libertarian candidate for governor of Vermont.

The libel action was brought by Attorney John A. Burgess, not to be confused with John S. Burgess who served as lieutenant governor. John A. was a 1960 graduate of Boston University Law School in the same class as F. Lee Bailey, as well as other Vermont attorneys Phyllis Armstrong, Gilbert Meyers, and Joe O'Rourke. The allegation was that George had filed a complaint with the real estate commission alleging that another broker had committed unspecified unethical acts. George had told me that he and the other realtor had both been trying to sell a piece of property. The other realtor had told the potential seller not to deal with George Trask's clients because they were black. This infuriated George's independent libertarian streak, and believing that such prejudices had no place in the marketplace, he filed a complaint with the state regulatory body. In his complaint he set out the facts of the particular incident, but also added that he had heard of other unethical acts by the same realtor. It was the last phrase that formed the basis for the lawsuit.

To put the claim in the context of the time, this was the age of the beginning of the civil rights movement. It was also a time when a lawyer could obtain a lien by a writ of attachment on someone's property merely by making a claim without having to show any validity in the claim. Burgess had filed such an attachment, claiming a lien of a half million dollars on all real property in which George Trask had an interest. This unilateral attachment practice was later abolished by a ruling of the United States Supreme Court which held that before such a writ of attachment could be granted, a judge would have to be convinced the claimant had the probability of success and that the amount of the attachment was reasonable.

One early summer day I drove to Newfane to draw a jury in the case. Before that, I had called Burgess and told him I thought his claim was frivolous, but because of the expenses involved in defending the matter, I would get my client to pay five hundred dollars to make it go away. We had what I believed to be good defenses to the claim. However, there was always the lingering remote danger that while George could defend his position with regard to the facts in the complaint he had made about the racist remarks of his fellow realtor—the facts were true—he might have a problem in substantiating his charge of other unethical acts he knew of only by rumor. It was not without some difficulty that I had gotten permission from George to make the five- hundred-dollar offer.

While we were waiting for our turn to draw the jury, Burgess asked me to step into the plaintiffs' witness room at the back of the courtroom, where he indicated to me that he had authority to reduce his client's demand from five hundred thousand to twenty-five thousand dollars. I told him this was ridiculous, and that I no longer had authority even to pay the five hundred, as my client had now had to pay me to come to Newfane. He went off to make a phone call and came back shortly saying he had talked to his client and was now able to reduce his demand to ten thousand dollars. I again reiterated my position that I had no authority to offer him anything at this point. He dropped his demand to five thousand, and I went to talk to my clients to see if they wanted to make a counter offer. George made it quite clear that this was now a matter of principle at this point, and the firm would not pay him a single penny. I informed Burgess of my client's decision, and he came back and said, "Well, get me twenty-five hundred dollars, and I'll tell my client I got five thousand and took half for my fee, and I'll go home." When once again I reiterated the position of my client, John dropped his demand to fifteen hundred. At this time I went back to my client and said, "We're now at a level when we have to think seriously about making an offer. There is always some risk of losing and the costs of trial would be in excess of the amount he is asking. You would be losing financially even if we won the case." George, sticking to his principles, refused to authorize me to make any offer, and I went back and told John Burgess that. He thought a minute and said, "All right, I'll take your offer of five hundred dollars." I told him I no longer had authority to pay five hundred dollars. He looked amazed and said, "But you offered that to me over the phone last week." I reminded him I had taken the offer off the table that morning. He then said, "Get me two hundred fifty dollars and I'll give it to my client, saying I kept the rest as a fee."

I told him I would go back once again to talk to my client.

This time, I took my client out of the courthouse onto the green in front of the courthouse and said, "I can't let you not settle this case. You're going to have to pay the two-fifty and get this business behind you." He again refused. I took him by the lapels and I said, "Don't be a fool. Let's get this case settled." He looked at me and said, "It's a matter of principle. I will not pay him two hundred fifty dollars," and then, after a short pause, continued, with a smile on his face, "Go offer him one twenty-five, and see what he says." I went back into the courthouse and told Burgess that I had authority to make an offer of one hundred and twenty-five dollars. He immediately accepted and went off to inform the court that the case was over. We had settled what had started out as a case with a lien on my client's property of five hundred thousand dollars, for one hundred twenty-five dollars. What Burgess told his client I can only speculate. This is the same John A. Burgess who was later convicted in California of embezzling millions of dollars of his clients' funds and who spent several years in the California prison system. I can only speculate on what he told those clients.

The Washington County Courthouse in Montpelier, with its white columns, looks a bit out of place on the north side of Main Street. It looks like a court designed for a rural town, not a state capital. It is now dwarfed by the federal courthouse and post office on its immediate west and business blocks on the east. While many famous persons have motored down Main Street past the courthouse to the state capital, it is not these vehicles nor their occupants that have captured the imagination of the local population.

Vermonters have taken to stock car racing much like rural people throughout the United States. A Vermont stock car racing tradition centers around a small asphalt racetrack in Barre known by the imposing name of Thunder Road. Thunder Road is the home of the annual Vermont Milk Bowl race where each year the winner has the responsibility of kissing a genuine Vermont Beauty, usually a Guernsey. After all, it is the Milk Bowl. It is equally famous for its amateur and beginning drivers, the Flying Tigers. Thunder Road was developed by stock car enthusiast Ken Squier. Ken is known to many

Americans throughout the country as a major voice on CBS Motor Sports, having been their featured race commentator for many years, broadcasting such events as the "Daytona 500." In January, 1978, Ken sold Thunder Road to another racetrack enthusiast by the name of Anastasias Kalomiris. Kalomiris's enthusiasm was not matched by his ability to manage a business. Soon the track was in trouble. It was deteriorating physically, the purses were not paid, and the payments on the mortgages to Thunder Road Enterprises and the First Vermont Bank & Trust Co. fell seriously in arrears. The bank started a foreclosure proceeding in November of 1978 in the Washington County Superior Court.

The trial court's first ruling in the case took a trip down the street to the Vermont Supreme Court which held that even though Thunder Road had redeemed the bank's mortgage, it had failed to file a cross-foreclosure on Kalomiris.[6] On remand from the Vermont Supreme Court, I was asked to try the case, which by now involved not only the original foreclosure, but a counterclaim by Kalomiris against Thunder Road.

In the interim between the trial court's order and the supreme court's decision, Squier and a new partner, Tom Curley, had regained control of the track. At trial Kalomiris took the stand and testified as to things he saw happening at the track during this period. Kalomiris had been banned from the track, and as he was well known to all the people at the gates, I asked him how he obtained this information. He told me he had entered the track on race days, had made inspections, and had seen these things for himself. My next question was, "How did you get into the track without being seen by any of the operating personnel?" He responded, "I came in disguise." I then asked him what his disguise was, and he said, "I took off my toupee." As he said that, he reached up with his left hand and took off his hair piece, exposing a bald head. My clients looked at each other and agreed between themselves that it had been an effective disguise.

Later that year at the annual NASCAR banquet, Ken Squier was acting as master of ceremonies. It was a real party with approximately five hundred people crowding into the grand ballroom of the Radisson Hotel in Burlington. There were trophies for every category imaginable dealing with the racing of the cars, their maintenance, and the pit crews who keep them going on race day. People came dressed in anything from Brooks Brothers suits to blue jeans and a tee shirt that didn't quite cover the stomach. The trophies themselves were golden obelisks, running from about a foot high to the championship trophy which looked at least five feet tall. A Freudian might suggest that the aggressive driving of stock car racing and its macho reputation deserved a trophy of phallic design.

During the course of his job as master of ceremonies, Ken Squier brought up the lawsuit, but instead of telling the tale of the removed toupee, he simply acknowledged that the case was won and that Thunder Road would remain in his and his new partner Tom Curley's hands for the immediate future. Cheers came up from the crowd again. He added that it was good to have the track back on the circuit with the assurance that the purse checks would be good once again. Cheers came up from the crowd. At this point, to my surprise, he said he would like to personally thank his attorney who had worked so hard to accomplish this result and asked me to stand. It was the only time in my life, and probably will be the only time in my life, when I saw a lawyer get a standing ovation from a stock car crowd. I felt as if I'd won a featured event . . . but I didn't get a trophy.

Bennington County is the only county in Vermont to have two separate courthouses, one in the town of Bennington and the other in the town of Manchester. The courthouse in Bennington is located on the west side of U.S. Route 7, just south of Main Street. It is a lovely old building with white columns in the front and a stairway just inside the front door leading up to the second floor courtroom. Light streams in from large windows on both sides of the courtroom, as it occupies the full width of the building. Here also is the home of the Samuel Blackmer Law Library. Blackmer, who died in 1953, was, in the opinion of many, the most brilliant justice ever to sit on the Vermont Supreme Court.

I ventured into this courthouse when Dr. Irving Lyons, a professor at Bennington College, claimed he was improperly denied presumptive tenure and he sued the college. Lyons's contract had expired and he sued not only the college for denying his tenure, but also past presidents of the college, Edward Bloustein and Harry W. Pearson. Donald K. Brown, who had served as an acting president, was also joined as a defendant, and all the individuals were accused of having interfered with Lyons' contractual rights to tenure. After the initial hearing, Superior Judge Edward Amidon granted the defendants' motion to dismiss the case, based on legal issues. Lyons took an appeal to the Vermont Supreme Court, which reversed some of Amidon's legal rulings and sent the case back for trial.[7]

After the case came back to the Bennington Superior Court and was set for trial, my partner, Mark Sperry, asked me to help him with it. We went off to Bennington, checked into the Paradise Motel, and the next day went to the courthouse for the jury draw.

The mechanics of the jury draw required the clerk to roll a wooden tumbler that held narrow paper strips, each containing the name of a potential juror. The clerk would pull twelve slips, one at a time, and as each name was called, that person took up a position in the jury box. The slip of paper would then be placed on a small wooden paddle. At that point the lawyers were given the opportunity to question the potential jurors. If a lawyer challenged one for bias, and the court agreed, the court would excuse that person, and the slip with the juror's name would be taken from the paddle. Another slip would be drawn from the tumbler, the new juror would take the empty seat in the jury box, and the slip would be placed in the vacant spot on the paddle. After the questioning was done and the court had decided the challenges for cause, each side was entitled to six peremptory challenges, each of which allows a lawyer to discard a juror for whatever reason the lawyer has, and without forcing the lawyer to explain what that might be. This causes a type of gamesmanship, as each side tries to reject jurors it perceives would be favorable to the other side. The ultimate goal in theory is to get as neutral a jury as can be found. Whether or not this really works is open to discussion. A cottage industry of experts has arisen trying to find jurors who are predisposed toward a client's position, and many millions of dollars have been spent by litigants hiring consultants to help them pick the type of person they think would be favorably disposed to their cause. We didn't have the luxury of funding for such consultants and were left solely to our own predilections. Even with the best of consultants and expertise in the selection of a jury such as O.J. Simpson had, there is an open question as to whether anyone can guess what a juror's predisposition would be. I learned that lesson well in this case.

When it came time for me to exercise my last peremptory challenge, I was tempted to pass. I had one lingering question. Juror number one, to my best guess, was Jewish. What stereotypes I used to come to that conclusion I have long since eradicated. The plaintiff was also Jewish. In trying to use the system in the best way possible to protect my client, I came to the conclusion that perhaps a Jewish juror would be more inclined to protect a Jewish plaintiff who had been rejected by the college. With an uneasy squeamishness in my stomach, I decided to use a peremptory challenge against Juror number one. I didn't feel good about my reasons, but under the pressures of making quick decisions, I decided not to take a risk. I exercised the challenge.

Carelessly, I withdrew the wrong name from the paddle. When the juror whose name that I had drawn was excused and asked to go to the back of the courtroom, the juror whom I intended to discharge was still sitting in the first row of the jury box.

At the conclusion of the judge's charge, a foreperson is appointed from among the jurors. The woman I had attempted to challenge was selected by the judge to be the foreperson. The clerk was instructed to hand the verdict slip, which was in an open envelope, to the foreperson, and the jurors were directed to retire for deliberation. The foreperson tucked the envelope under her arm and marched out with the jury. Twenty minutes later she marched back into the courtroom with the verdict form sealed in the envelope, once again tucked under her arm. When the verdict was opened and read in open court, we had won.

In reflecting on the moment, I now realize that not only had I attempted to reject a juror for wrong reasons, but I had also completely misunderstood where that juror might be coming from. I had never had a jury come back quite so dramatically and in such a short time. Ever since, I have been more than a bit skeptical when lawyers tell how their experience in selecting juries and their judgment in this regard are all–important in the decision of the case. While I will admit that jurors bring with them certain baggage, my experiences tell me they take their jobs seriously, and it's the facts of the case that almost always control the outcome, not individual biases.

AN ASIDE

Donald Brown was one of Bennington's favorite faculty members and lived with his wife and family on a farm just a few miles north of the college. Here they had a small flock of sheep, and combined the best of a farm homestead and an academic community. During the course of the trial, Don had come to me and said, "Peter, is there any possibility I will lose my farm and home in the course of this case?" I told him there was no reasonable possibility that this could happen, as even if the plaintiff won, there would have to be a judgment that Bennington College could not satisfy before they could look to him for payment. Besides, their home farm was in both his and his wife's name, and as only he had been sued, a judgment against him could not reach an asset which was held by both of them. I told him, "The chance of your losing the farm is somewhat less than being struck by lightning."

As lightning does in fact strike people, he became convinced that there was a real possibility he would lose everything. Remember, he was an academic. Thereafter, from his viewpoint, we took on the principal role as defenders of his homestead, with the protection of the college as a secondary consideration. During the course of the trial, the Browns invited my partner and me to their farm for dinner. It turned out that the year before one of their daughters had been diagnosed with a brain tumor. She had gone on a ying-yang microbiotic diet hoping for remission and her parents joined in the diet in support of her cure. Whether the diet worked or not, the young lady did have a remission and survived the diagnosed brain cancer. Thus, at the time we were invited to dinner, the Browns were committed vegetarians. However, as sheep farmers, they prepared for us a wonderful platter of lamb chops. Since the time I was old enough to chew meat, I have been a consummate meat eater. In our dinner conversations, I was explaining to the Browns that I usually eat meat two to three times a day. I further jokingly explained that I had a great passion for beef and lamb, as I felt red meat made me more aggressive. To me the conversation was little more than a capricious table conversation. Suddenly, however, Mrs. Brown's eyes lit up, she grabbed the platter of lamb chops, and said, "Can I help you to some more meat?" I looked at her as I helped myself, and then started laughing, as we both realized the instinct that she had succumbed to was "feed that tiger."

Another case brought me to the second Bennington County Courthouse, located in Manchester.

Hard cash was a scarce commodity in Vermont during the 1930s. It was still a time when Vermont was dominated by agriculture, and Vermont agriculture was dominated by family dairy farms. One such farm was located on Nichols Hill in the town of Dorset. It was owned by John W. and Ada Nichols. Even during the great depression, with the help of their eight children, they managed to keep everybody clothed and fed. Their fifteen year old son, John Nichols, Jr., Junior as he was known, was off at technical school in Randolph when in 1938 his father died.

Junior came home from school and took on the challenge of managing the farm. Despite his youth, he had learned a lot about farming, was a willing and hard worker, and managed to meet the responsibilities of running the farm. He even did extra work off the farm and put his earnings into its operation. As he turned eighteen, he began to think of the world beyond the farm, and considered moving on to make a career for himself. His mother took him aside and told him that if he would stay and run the farm, providing for herself and the younger children as they grew up, the farm would someday be his. Based on this promise, he gave up thoughts of leaving, married Ethel in 1942, and for forty years farmed the property.

Over the years day in and day out, with twice daily chores of milking, growing of crops, harvesting, repairing machinery, and a million and one other tasks, he provided for his mother and for the younger children. In 1958, he became concerned that the farm was still in his mother's name, and while he had her promise, he had nothing in writing that would protect him if anything happened to her. He made arrangements to seek the advice of an attorney in Manchester, and a deed was prepared giving him title to the main farm. But the deed omitted a second parcel known as the Chancellor Allen tract. His mother assured him that eventually he would get the Allen tract as well. He continued farming and caring for the premises until his mother's death in 1978.

Shortly after her death, Junior came in to see me to inquire what he should do about getting the Allen tract. It had been promised to him, but a second deed had never been signed. I told him to talk with his seven brothers and sisters to see if they were agreeable to living up to their mother's promise. Surprisingly, instead of agreeing to respect their mother's promise, they took the position that not only were they entitled to their share of the Allen tract, but they also wanted their share of the main farm that had already been conveyed to him and Ethel. They claimed that when he acquired the main farm in 1958 their mother was incompetent.

The seven siblings hired Art O'Dea, later to become a superior judge, and still later to become known as Vermont's most active mediator. He brought suit on their behalf asking that the main farm be transferred back from Junior and his wife to his mother's estate and distributed equally among all her children. Junior filed a counterclaim asking that the interest in the Allen tract held in the estate be decreed to himself and Ethel pursuant to the contract he and his mother had entered into. He maintained he had fully completed his end of the contract by caring both for his brothers and sisters as they grew up, and for his mother until the time of her death.

The case came on for trial in the Bennington County Courthouse that lies on the town square in Manchester. It is a small courthouse located adjacent to a church and across from the Equinox House. It is a picturesque setting many people admire when driving on U.S. Route 7. The trial was before Judge Stephen Martin, the chief superior judge. Despite the fact the case was really an equity case where there is no right to a jury, Judge Martin decided to submit questions to an advisory jury, which acts like any other jury, but only advises the judge on the facts, the judge ultimately making the decision. Susan Humphrey, a bright and perceptive associate, tried the case with me. The courthouse was a long commute from our office in Middlebury, and we stayed in Manchester. After a long day in trial, we would sneak off to fly fish on the famous Battenkill. We joked that we hoped we would have better results with the jury than we had with the fish.

AN ASIDE

Shortly after the trial, Susan married Max Eaton, an upcoming young businessman in Middlebury. After the birth of their second child, she took an extended maternity leave. Late one afternoon, toward the end of that leave, she arrived at my office. She told me she had decided to leave the practice of law to become a full-time mother. She then produced a bottle of Glenlivet, which we opened and then toasted her new career. I told her I was saving the rest of the bottle for another toast when she would decide to return to the practice. That bottle is still in my office closet, waiting for that occasion.

We closed the evidence portion of the Nichols trial early Thursday afternoon and the court recessed until Friday morning for closing arguments, the judge's charge, and jury deliberations. Susan and I had been discussing the case and trying to figure out what would be the best approach to take during closing argument. I was reminded of the children's story, *The Little Red Hen*. There seemed a parallel between the seven brothers and sisters who were unavailable to take on the responsibilities when Junior took over the working of the farm, but yet wanted to reap the benefits of that endeavor after forty years of his work. Thursday afternoon we made our way to the children's section of the bookstore in Manchester in an attempt to buy a copy of the story of *The Little Red Hen*. They didn't have a copy. Walking back up the street toward the courthouse, I noticed the town library, and on a hunch we went in. Sure enough, they had a battered old copy which they allowed us to check out for the next day.

Art O'Dea as plaintiffs' counsel made the first argument, doing a good job laying out his clients' claims carefully. His seven clients were sitting in the front row of the spectators' gallery on the south side of the courthouse, the side closest to where the jury sat, eating up his every word. When my time came to close, I approached the jury waving the battered library book in my hand. I started out by saying, "Who was there when it came time to plant in 1938?" I looked and pointed down the row at the seven siblings, almost as if they had been staged as a prop for my next statement. 'Not I,' said the seven children." I then looked away and turned to the jury, and said, "But who was there when the time came to reap?" I again looked at the seven brothers and sisters in the front row, who by this time were beginning to look somewhat confused and, perhaps in my eyes, a bit guilty. A woman juror in the front row smiled and chuckled to herself, and I felt perhaps I had hit upon the right theme. After an appropriate pause, I went on to the rest of my argument which was rather short and to the point. I called upon the jury to reject the siblings' claim of their mother's incompetence in favor of a completion of the bargain which Junior had entered into and had faithfully fulfilled.

Art O'Dea had a chance for rebuttal, but there was not much he could do with the tattered library book lying on the defendants' table. He tried briefly and sat down. Judge Martin then charged the jury, describing the duties of jurors as to how to handle the evidence, the part of the charge which lawyers call "boilerplate," explaining the particular law applicable to the facts of this case, and detailing the jurors' specific responsibilities in dealing with the mechanics of rendering a verdict.

The court officer, a bailiff, sitting on the north side of the courthouse across from the jury, and in close proximity to the defense table, was a wonderful old fellow who stood about five foot two. He had traveled with circuses as an animal trainer for many years, and he had a sharp sense of humor. The judge got into that part of the charge where he was reciting the law of the case, and at a point where he was starting to explain the circumstances under which my client would be entitled to win, the clarion bells of the church next door started playing, and as the judge delivered his words, celestial music wafted through the windows lining the north side of the courthouse, celestial music surreptitiously softly filling the courtroom. The bailiff, who was sitting only about five feet away from my table, scribbled a note and handed it to me. I carefully opened it so as not to distract the attention of the jurors from the judge's charge. It read: "For five dollars I'll get you a special musical request."

The jury deliberated for only an hour and a half before they reached a verdict. They agreed with Junior and answered the questions that had been submitted, letting him keep the main farm, and ordering the Allen tract, still in the name of the mother's estate, to be decreed to him. The case was appealed to the Vermont Supreme Court, where the decision of the jury was affirmed.[8]

9.

SPEEDING

In the early 1960s there was no radar in Vermont. Speeders were usually apprehended by a state police officer who would follow them over a distance of miles, pull them over, and charge them with the speed observed through the pursuit. After 1965, as I reversed my role from prosecutor to defense counsel, stationary radar came into use. Stationary radar seemed like a magical box located in a side window of a state police cruiser, the cruiser usually being hidden along the side of the road. It was claimed that this magic box could measure the speed of vehicles coming toward it. The first radar machines printed out a piece of paper with a number on it indicating the speed of the vehicle it had supposedly focused on.

On one occasion, a man came into my office and said he had been given a citation to appear in court for going seventy-eight miles per hour in a fifty mile per hour zone. When asked if an officer clocked him, he said, "No." The officer had used radar and had shown him a slip of paper with the number 78 on it. I told him I would defend him.

I was sure the police officer involved had no idea how radar worked and had no more training than to point it, press a button, and read the piece of paper that the machine printed. If the only evidence the state could produce was this piece of paper with the number 78 marked on it and the state had no one to explain how the machine worked, then the burden of proving the case beyond a reasonable doubt would not have been met, and the client would be entitled to an acquittal.

In the 1960s, a speeding case was treated like any other misdemeanor and had to be prosecuted by an "information." An information is a formal charging document. It starts out with the statement that it is being brought by the state's attorney under oath of office, and after stating the substance of the crime charged ends with the words "and against the peace and dignity of the state." There were no traffic courts and no traffic tickets. The alleged speeder was also entitled to a twelve-person jury as a matter of right, and in this case, we insisted upon it. At trial, presided over by Judge William S. Burrage, the police officer took the stand and told the jury of the location of his vehicle. He testified as to turning on the machine, testing it with a tuning fork (the same as used by a piano tuner), seeing my client's car coming, pressing a button, and receiving the piece of paper showing the number 78.

Under cross-examination, he admitted he had no idea how the radar worked and that he had received instruction only on how to operate it. The roll-top desk of the county clerk stood in front of the bench on the other side of the courtroom from the jury. On it there was a number stamp the clerk used for marking docket numbers. When pressed down, it printed a number in large, bold, black ink. I had previously set the number on the stamp at 78. I took it from the desk and handed it to the officer along with a piece of paper. I asked him to push down on the stamp to make an impression on the paper. He obliged, and sure enough, there was the number 78 in its full glory. To the next question, "Does that mean a car was going seventy-eight miles per hour?" he quite brightly pointed out, "Of course not." On further examination, he couldn't explain the scientific connection between the number 78 on the piece of paper in his file and the allegations that the defendant's vehicle was going seventy-eight miles per hour.

Despite growls from Judge Burrage, not known to favor the defense, the client was acquitted. It was well known that the Commissioner of Motor Vehicles often used his broad discretion to suspend licenses of even first-time speeders and that, coupled with the fact that the defendant was a long-distance truck driver, may have played a more important role in his ultimate acquittal than the paper stamped 78 by the clerk's number stamp.

With my confidence bolstered, I decided to try to defend a second radar case. Knowing Judge Burrage was not pleased with the verdict in the first case and would probably cut off a repeat use of the number stamp, I decided to use a slightly different tack but followed the same basic defense, that the officer did not know the science of how radar worked. The police officer testifying was Corporal Lee Jones, the head of the Middlebury barracks, who, after his retirement from the state police, became a long-standing and respected sheriff for Rutland County. Lee testified to the positioning of his vehicle, the setting up of the radar gun, and his ultimate determination that the radar had caught the client speeding fifteen miles over the speed limit.

When the time came for cross-examination, I pulled from my briefcase a copy of a children's book, the *Dr. Seuss Dictionary*. I had the court reporter mark the inside cover with a yellow exhibit sticker, "Defendant's #1." I handed the book to Lee Jones and asked him to identify it. He said, "Why this is a *Dr. Seuss Dictionary*." I asked if he would turn to Page M and tell me what he saw. On Page M there was an illustration of a complicated machine with bells, whistles, chutes, and anything else that Dr. Seuss's imagination could put into a contraption, calling it a machine. Lee said, "It's a machine, I guess." I asked him this: "If I were to tell you that machine could measure the speed of a vehicle, would you accept it on faith as you had done with the radar machine?" At this time, Ezra Dike, the state's attorney, objected, and Judge Burrage upheld the objection and quite clearly told me to put the children's book back into my briefcase. Undaunted, I asked the next question, "Have you ever seen a Rube Goldberg cartoon of a machine?" Dike was quick to his feet, again objecting. Judge Burrage sustained the objection saying, "We'll have no more of those antics in this courtroom." I moved on to another line of inquiry.

This time the jury returned a verdict of guilty. As my three children grew up and looked at their *Doctor Seuss Dictionary*, they asked, "Daddy, what is that yellow sticker on the front page for?"

This did not end my career as a defender of lead-footed drivers. When John Masterson was elected State's Attorney, he decided to save himself some office time, so instead of individually preparing an

"Information" for each person charged with a motor-vehicle offense, he had a form printed with all the various traffic charges listed. In front of each listing was a box for a check mark. Charles Edward Chapman was charged with speeding under such an Information. Judge Burrage denied my motion to dismiss the Information as being ambiguous and not conforming to the Vermont Constitution, and allowed the state to go to trial with that particular charging document. The jury convicted Chapman, and then Judge Burrage denied the post verdict motion "in arrest of judgment," which was the formal way to challenge once again the form of the Information, even after the verdict. Feeling simpatico with the convicted defendant and somewhat frustrated by Burrage's pro state posture, I undertook an appeal of the case to the Vermont Supreme Court.

In an opinion by Justice Percival L. Shangraw, the supreme court reversed the denial of the motion for arrest of judgment and sent the state packing, saying,

> The information contains several printed offenses. The "x" inserted in the box or square preceding the speeding charge, of which respondent was convicted, is the only indication contained in the information to apprise the respondent on which of the several charges he was to stand trial. The remaining printed offenses were not deleted.

> Again referring to the form and substance of the information, it must be admitted that except by a studied examination of the information by a person fully familiar with the significance, effect, and meaning of the "x" inserted in the square in question, a grave doubt would arise in the mind of a respondent as to which of the several alleged offenses he must be prepared to meet. For this reason it lacks certainty and particularity, and does not meet the standard required by Ch. 1, Art. 10 of the Vermont Constitution.[9]

Was the fact that Masterson never briefed the case or even showed up for oral argument the determining factor on the appeal or was Justice Shangraw really concerned about the ambiguity of "x"?

In another speeding case, one that almost made its way to the supreme court, Judge Burrage had ruled that radar had become a sufficiently accepted method of apprehending speeders, that it was not necessary for the state to call an expert witness to explain how it worked, and the court could take judicial notice that radar, if properly operated, could in fact detect speeders and was admissible as evidence, even without an explanation to the jury of how it scientifically worked. Judge Burrage's ruling in allowing judicial notice to be taken of the workings of radar was based on the fact that he simply did not think speed was a serious enough offense to merit the call for a scientific explanation. I suggested, but to no avail, that if the same quality of evidence were offered in a murder case, no judge would let facts be found based upon judicial notice rather than expert scientific testimony. This put to rest, or almost put to rest, my defense of persons charged with speeding through the use of radar.

AN ASIDE

Anthony Doria, the founder of Vermont Law School as a proprietary law school, later took the question to the Vermont Supreme Court in a case where he was convicted of speeding based on radar. The Vermont Supreme Court in its wisdom agreed that judicial notice could be taken[10] of the effectiveness and accuracy of radar, and scientific proof would not be required as to how it actually operated.

There was, however, one case which never actually made it to court. It involved the prosecution of a local minister for allegedly going eighty miles per hour on the new Vermont interstate section between Montpelier and Burlington. The section of the road on which the speeding supposedly took place was in Chittenden County, and thus under the jurisdiction of State's Attorney Patrick Leahy. The minister was wearing the cloth of his profession and said he was very careful about his speed and he was in no way going over the sixty-five miles-per-hour speed limit. The radar must be wrong. When asked if he was prepared to testify to that under oath, he said he was.

I called Pat and told him of my client's proposed testimony, and made the suggestion that a jury trial in this case would be a great test of "the cloth" versus "science." Apparently, not looking forward to the proposition of accusing a man of the cloth of testifying falsely in a case, and recognizing that even though radar was usually accurate it might once in a while make a mistake, Pat used his discretion and decided not to bring the case.

Of course, the discretion of whether to prosecute or not to prosecute a speeding case is usually in the hands of the officer who makes the stop. Today an officer has the choice of giving a warning or issuing a traffic ticket. In 1964 there were no traffic tickets and the officer could give a citation to come to court, but he (there were no women state troopers in 1964) had to discuss each case with the State's Attorney and convince the State's Attorney to issue an Information, charging the potential defendant with breaking the speed limit.

Stan Merriman was a young trooper whose first assignment was to the Middlebury barracks. Stan had an instinct for ferreting out all types of criminal activity. He was also zealous in his enforcement of traffic laws, especially speeding. One day he came in and asked me, as State's Attorney, to issue an Information for a person he had cited for speeding. He said that when he had been patrolling the section of Route 7 between Salisbury and Leicester known as Salisbury Flats, he came upon two vehicles, each going in excess of seventy miles an hour, and he pulled them both over. I asked him why, if he had stopped two vehicles, he wanted an Information against only one of them. Stan replied that he had given the first guy the citation for speeding and then had walked back to the second car, with the full intention of doing the same to the other driver. When he got to the second car, he saw this attractive young woman who had rolled her window down. As he came to her car, she pulled her shoulders together towards the front, and looking up at Stan, said, "Yes, officer." She was wearing a soft blue sweater and no bra. Stan related that and added, "Peter, I just couldn't bring myself to give her a citation." Discretion works in wondrous ways.

AN ASIDE

Stan, in the early 70s, after having been transferred out of Addison County, came back as an undercover agent for the narcotics division of the state police. On one occasion he was visiting an abandoned quarry in Leicester which had filled with water and, being remote, was used as a nude-swimming hole by the flower children of the day. Stan also believed a great deal of marijuana was being smoked there. He decided that in order to blend into the surroundings in his position as an undercover cop, he would have to shed his clothing and join the group in the buff. Unfortunately for Stan, and perhaps fortunately for the assemblage there, as he took off his pants, a set of handcuffs fell out of his pocket and tumbled down the stones towards the edge of the quarry. While he recovered his handcuffs before they met the depths of the water, his cover at that locale was permanently blown.

Police discretion crosses state boundaries. Once when a group of us were heading to Cape Cod on a fishing trip, the car I was driving was being followed by a second car driven by Francis O'Brien. As we reached the interstate system in New Hampshire, Francis got a little anxious and decided I wasn't traveling quite fast enough. He passed me and started going along at quite a clip. I decided his pace was a little fast and that I would eventually catch up to him, so I kind of eased it along. About ten miles down the road I sure did catch up with him. He was pulled over to the side with a New Hampshire State Trooper parked behind him, his lights flashing. I drove in front of them, stopped the car, and went back to Francis to see if with my legal skills I might be of any help. As I approached the car, Francis waved me back to my car, and I heard the police officer say, "Reverend, I'll let you go on your way, but do please slow down."

10.

COSTUMES

A jury's first impression of a lawyer or of a witness is visual and can be very important. Part of that first impression is formed by the costume the person is wearing. Juries expect lawyers to be dressed appropriately. A lawyer dressed in a conservative suit, polished shoes, and an attractive tie, or in a conservative dress or business outfit, will have a different effect on a jury from someone who is wearing khaki pants and a sports jacket, or slacks and a sweater. A man with a ponytail or shoulder length hair creates a different impression than does someone with a military crewcut. Each costume has its place, and careful consideration is often given as to how the lawyer or the witness wishes to appear before a jury. Obviously, the costume forms only an initial view of the individual and is only a part of the whole picture that will be seen by the jury in the course of a trial. It is important that witnesses feel comfortable in their chosen costume.

On some occasions the lawyer has little control over what a witness will wear. On one occasion in a trial in Brattleboro where my client was charged with robbery, we were faced with an unusual occurrence. My client had been charged with using threats of force to make a tenant in one of his apartments write a check for some overdue rent. The state felt this came within the robbery statute, and he was charged with a felony. After receiving the check, my client went down to the local branch of the bank to deposit it, while the alleged victim called the bank to put a stop order on the check. As in most lawsuits, in this case there was a difference in the testimony as to what had actually transpired. As the morning session of the trial drew to a close, it became apparent to me that I was going to need to call a bank officer who had knowledge of the sequence of events. As soon as the lunch break began, I drove to the bank, armed with a subpoena for a vice president, the person who had the information we needed. What I had forgotten was that it was Halloween.

I arrived at the bank to find everyone in costume. When I was finally introduced to the vice president, I found her to be wearing a full-blown clown costume. She had red Raggedy Ann hair, a bulbous nose, a full clown costume with a hooped belly, and very large duck-like yellow shoes that forced her to waddle when walking. I gave her the subpoena and told her to be in court in approximately forty-five minutes. She said she would not have time to go home to change her clothes and meet that deadline. I explained to her the deadline was more important than what she was wearing, and she would just have to come to court dressed as a clown.

As the court reconvened at 1:30, she entered the courtroom and sat in the back row. The jury, Judge Paul Hudson, and everyone else in the courtroom turned to look as she sat down. Judge Hudson told me to call my next witness.

"My next witness will be the vice president of the bank." She rose from her seat in the back of the room and, with her oversized yellow duck feet, came waddling forward to take her position in the witness box. There she was before the jury in full clown dress. While there were smiles as she approached the witness box, no one quite knew what was coming. The oath was administered and she sat down. My first question was to ask her her name. This question was followed by what was her occupation. She answered those questions straightfor-wardly. I then asked her "Do you always dress this way?" She gave me a withering look that extended far beyond her bulbous nose, and said, "No, only on Halloween." She finished her testimony, and despite her costume, her integrity was never challenged by the jury.

One day in the early 1970s, a relatively minor matter took me to the courthouse in Hyde Park, the county seat of Lamoille County. It is a rural Vermont town, with the courthouse located on the west side of the one street running through the village. It is about a two-hour drive north from Middlebury, and on this particular day, John Legault, a partner in some real estate ventures with me, agreed to take a ride to see the scenery and to have a chance to talk about several matters we had pending. We never expected to see what confronted us when we climbed the broad staircase to the second story and the old courtroom itself.

On entering the courtroom, we saw, sitting in the front row of the benches in the spectator's section on the north side of the court-house, a man dressed in a baseball uniform with his hand and his head wrapped in bandages. Both his wrists and legs were shackled and there was a deputy sheriff sitting on each side of him.

The court took his case first as was the usual practice for a defen-dant who was in custody. The judge read the charge, arson, an attempt to burn down a local motel. He entered a plea of not guilty, and the question of setting bail arose. The prosecutor stepped forward and told the following tale: the defendant, who was from the Boston area, had come up the night before. In order to ensure that his per-sonal vehicle not be identified in connection with his planned escapade, he had stolen a pickup truck. In the early morning hours of the day we were in court, he had taken the stolen pickup, along with two five gallon cans of gasoline, and driven to the rear of a motel he intended to set fire to. He went into the motel, poured the gasoline throughout the building, and lit a match. There was an explosion, and his clothes caught on fire. He came running out of the motel building trying to put out the fire on his clothes, swatting them with his hands, and rolling on the ground. While still smoldering, he jumped into the stolen pickup truck, and took off down the road. Both the fire depart-ment and the sheriff's department responded to calls about the explo-sion and the resulting fire. A deputy sheriff approaching the motel noticed a pickup truck heading away from the fire at great speed. He decided to give pursuit. As the would-be arsonist came to a "T" in the road, he tried to make the corner, lost control and drove into and partway out the other side of a barn located at the intersection.

Although banged up by the accident, the defendant jumped out of the truck and started to run through the woods. The deputy sheriff, who had radioed for help, pulled his cruiser up to where the pickup had met the barn, and then, with another officer soon joining him, took after the defendant on foot. The defendant was shortly brought to ground by the two officers and was taken into custody. After being given medical assistance for his burns, he was taken to the Lamoille County Jail, a building located next to the courthouse. That same afternoon he was due in court for his arraignment. As his clothes had been burned, the sheriffs had to find something that he could wear to the courthouse. The only thing they had was the old baseball uniform.

The state's attorney informed the court that this man was an arsonist who had been hired to come up from Boston to burn down the building, that he had a long criminal record, and that bail should be set at one hundred thousand dollars. In response, the defendant interjected that the one hundred thousand dollar bail requested was out of the question and unnecessary, as he would certainly appear at any future proceeding. He then went on to say that a look at his record would indicate he had always appeared in court when he was supposed to. He added that, on one occasion he had been charged with murder, quickly pointing out that this resulted in a conviction of only manslaughter, and even then he had always appeared voluntarily.

While there may have been some logic to his position, it was not received with great joy by the court. The judge set bail at two hundred thousand dollars. The sheriff's deputies escorted the bandaged ballplayer down the courthouse steps and back to jail.

More than a quarter of a century later, I was visiting with John Legault who had since moved to Florida. He asked me if the practice was still as interesting as in the days of the bandaged ballplayer arsonist.

Often in cartoons, as well as occasionally in movies, there are scenes where a woman shows up at a fancy ball dressed in a gown she thought was an original only to find another woman there wearing the same dress. In the cartoons, daggers usually extend from the eyes of each individual as she perceives the other in what she believed to be her special prerogative, an original ball gown. In the movies, the daggers are absent, but the expressions on the faces of the parties tell the same story.

In 1972 I was to argue a motion in a murder case in an attempt to reduce a sentence that had been handed down in 1967. The state's attorney of Chittenden County was Patrick Leahy and the hearing was to be held in Burlington at the Chittenden County Courthouse. The courthouse, which has since burned down, was a large, old, redstone building located just south of where the converted Customs House building now houses the Chittenden Superior Court.

As it was an important case which had caught the attention of the press, I put on my best costume. I had just purchased a Stanley Blackmer double-breasted designer suit at Magram's Department Store on Church Street. Magram's had just expanded to include a men's clothing line and was the first store in Vermont to deal in "men's fashions." The suit was dark blue with a pin stripe, and was rather distinctive. I thought I looked like the epitome of a successful young lawyer wearing it. At exactly the moment when I walked into the main courtroom from the defendants' room located in the southeast corner of the second floor of the courthouse, Pat Leahy was entering the courtroom from the north side. We both looked up, and to our mutual amazement realized we were wearing brand-new, identical suits. I can't say daggers shot from our eyes, but we sure were surprised. Neither of us had one-upped the other in men's fashion.

On the motion, Judge Stephen Martin, the trial judge, ruled in my favor reducing the sentence from thirty-five to forty years to ten to forty years. On appeal, the Vermont Supreme Court, by a vote of four-to-one, ruled that the trial court did not have the power to change its sentence more than five years after it had been handed down. There was a dissent by Justice Albert Barney, then an associate justice, and later chief justice of the court. "A minimum of thirty-five years as applied to a sentence of forty years, it seems to me, brings maximum and minimum so close together, in the light of the length of the sentence, as to come substantively close to improving maximum and minimum sentences. This has already been held to be improper . . ."[11]

And then there is the case of the unintended costume. Michael Wool, one of my partners, served as City Grand Juror of Burlington in the early 1970s. The role of the city grand juror was to prosecute misdemeanors that occurred in Burlington. Mike was a life-long resident of the city and known to all the court personnel, especially Judge Edward Costello. Judge Costello knew the genealogy of not only every lawyer who appeared before him, but virtually every defendant who had been reared in Burlington and made his way into his court.

Mike had served as city grand juror for several months, disposing of all his cases without going to a jury trial. However, the time came when he had to appear for his first jury draw. It was held in the big courtroom of the district courthouse located on Pearl Street.

In all young lawyers, and most older lawyers, the nerves hit when it is time to draw a jury. Nerves affect different lawyers in different ways, but none are immune. Bernard Leddy (who later served as U.S. District Judge for the District of Vermont) used to throw up each morning before he entered the courtroom for a jury trial. Asa Bloomer, one of Vermont's all-time great trial lawyers, never ate lunch during trial, and could handle only a glass of milk. Mike's nervous problems were just the opposite. He got a bad case of the runs.

Just prior to his case being called for the jury draw, he had gone into the public washroom on the second floor of the courthouse and sat down. However, before sitting down, he had done what his mother had always taught him to do in using a strange bathroom, and that was line the seat with toilet paper. He was still sitting there when Judge Costello dispatched the bailiff to go find Mr. Wool to bring him into the courtroom to get the case moving. The bailiff found Mike in the bathroom stall and said he better get the hell in the courtroom as the judge was getting impatient. Mike, mindful of the bailiff's comments, quickly finished his business, pulled up his pants, and proceeded directly to the courtroom. The back benches of the courtroom were filled with potential jurors and, as Michael walked by them towards the counsel table, there was a slight titter among them. As he turned, Judge Costello could see the cause of the humor. He called Michael to the bench and explained that proper attire in his courtroom did not include a two-foot tail of toilet paper hanging down from his pants under his jacket to almost his knees. Michael quickly removed the offending strip, everybody had a good laugh, and the case went forward.

Unintended costumes don't always occur just in court. Jim Carroll, a Middlebury attorney, was on his way to his first real estate closing at a local bank. He was all excited as this was his first time to have the full responsibility for protecting his client in the purchase of some real estate. There is a major difference between primary participation in a closing, and just watching somebody else take responsibility when your role is simply to assist in the shuffling of papers for the person in charge.

Jim had a pen in hand as he jumped behind the wheel of his vehicle, turned on some music, and started driving to the bank. He became quite engaged with the music and happily tapped out time with his pen on the steering wheel. Just as he arrived at the bank with no time to spare, he started seeing black spots on the windshield. He looked around inside the car, and splattered all over the front seat and ceiling were black spots. He then looked down at his new summer suit and sure enough there were black spots all over it. He looked in the mirror and realized that his face had acquired black freckles.

With no time to return home to change, he had no choice but to go to the closing, sporting his newly formed freckles. And though his new costume did nothing to diminish the quality of his legal work, he felt a little less in charge of the situation than he might have been had he not gotten quite so wrapped up in the music.

Another unintended facial costume played a role in the trial of a land condemnation case. If the state highway department can prove the public interest is served by the taking of land along a highway, they can take it even over the objection of the landowner. In such a case both the U.S. Constitution and the Vermont Constitution require that owners of the condemned property shall be paid just compensation for the value of the land taken. Oftentimes the state appraiser and the landowner whose property is being taken disagree as to the value of the condemned parcel. The difference in value can ultimately be resolved by a jury. They determine the amount of just compensation.

In one condemnation case, Assistant Attorney General Thomas A. McCormick was counsel for the state of Vermont. His expert, a qualified real estate appraiser, testified that the property taken had only a minimal value and further that the taking did not reduce the value of the remainder of the property. The landowner, a farmer, was going to testify on his own behalf as to what he thought the condemned parcel was worth and how the remainder of his property was affected by the taking.

When he arrived in court, it was obvious that he was an old-time Vermonter who worked hard and worked outdoors. The trial was held during the summer, and when the farmer walked to the witness stand, anyone could see that when he worked outside he always wore a hat. His face was well tanned from the neck up to a line of powder-white skin which showed where the hat came down on his forehead. As Tom looked at the farmer standing before the witness chair taking the oath, he asked himself: "How do you cross-examine somebody with a halo?" The jury's verdict was exactly what the farmer asked for.

A lesson about costumes as well as other lessons came out of a trial in St. Albans. In 1966 the Franklin District Court was held in a corner room on the second floor of City Hall, located on Main Street. The room wasn't any larger than twenty-four feet square. It was by far the smallest courtroom in Vermont in which jury trials were conducted. The presiding judge was Carl Gregg, a tall, distinguished looking jurist, but no friend of a defendant. He was known as a hanging judge.

Ronald Rich had been apprehended at shotgun point by a local farmer. The farmer had found him with the nozzle from the farm's gas pump in the opening of the gas tank to his car. Mr. Rich was trying to work the hand pump to get fuel into the car. However, the handle had become tangled with wire the farmer had used in an attempt to lock the pump. The police had been called, and when they arrived, they found things unchanged, Rich at the wrong end of a shotgun and the fuel nozzle still in the car. They took the young Mr. Rich into custody, charging him with petty larceny.

The state's attorney was Ronald Kilburn (later a district judge) and this was going to be his first jury trial. Rich's only defense was that he had never actually obtained any gas, having been apprehended before the gas had started to flow, and therefore, there was no actual larceny. He might have been properly charged with an attempted petty larceny but the state failed to do this, and the court ruled that the case should go to the jury on the question of whether there had actually been a larceny or not.

As we started trial, Judge Gregg was on the bench. Immediately in front of the bench there were two small tables with three chairs. The tables were about the size of a card table. The state had the table at the left facing the bench, with one chair, and two feet to the right was the defense counsel's table with two chairs. Along the left wall was the jury box where twelve jurors were seated in as close quarters as you could imagine. Immediately behind where the attorneys sat there was a rail and behind that there were benches that could hold twelve to fifteen spectators.

The atmosphere in the tight confinement of the courtroom was rather tense. The new state's attorney, about to try his first jury trial, was tense; Judge Gregg was always tense in conducting any criminal proceeding; and my client was tense worrying about possibly going to jail. The fact that the entire courtroom was painted an institutional gray did nothing to lighten up the atmosphere.

The twelve potential jurors were drawn and the time came to use the preemptory challenges that each side had. The number two juror in the front row was a very attractive woman in her early twenties. For some reason I did not know then, and still do not know, when the bailiff passed the juror list to counsel for the exercise of the first peremptory challenge, State's Attorney Kilburn excused the number two juror. I decided this was my opportunity to lighten up the proceedings a little bit. Without a word, I stood up, and looking as stern as possible, walked over to the state's attorney's table and then, in a low whisper that only he could hear, I said, "Don't you know it's an unwritten constitutional rule that you never kick a good-looking woman off a jury?" Kilburn first was taken aback, and then slowly smiled. I returned to my seat, leaving everyone in the courtroom to guess what our conversation had been about. Such a comment today would not find much sympathy with my women partners. Times have changed.

When the evidence closed, the time came for closing arguments. After the state rested, I stood before the jury in the small courtroom wearing a bow tie, and told them, pointing my finger in an attempt at an authoritative gesture, that it was their duty to acquit, because the state had failed to prove that my client had actually accomplished the intended theft. The jury deliberated for about three hours before bringing back a verdict of guilty. Any appellate issues we had in mind vanished when the judge decided to give a probationary sentence rather than send my client to jail.

About two weeks later I attended a sensitivity training workshop at the Vermont State Hospital under the leadership of a psychologist, Bill Dean. The workshop was intended to bring people together from different walks of life, professionals, social workers, correction guards, and police officers, to help them get an idea of how other people perceive them and how people react in certain stress situations. In the course of the first day's session, I mentioned this trial and its outcome. Dean seized upon it as a teaching tool and had me reargue the case before twelve of the participants acting as jurors. I did my best and the twelve were sent off to deliberate. They came back shortly with a guilty verdict. There was then an opportunity to question the mock jurors as to how they reacted to my argument. I learned two things: One, they did not like being told what to do; and two, they didn't like my bow tie. Since then I have never worn a bow tie before a jury. There are a number of people who just react adversely to a bow tie as appearing too autocratic or upper crust, and this doesn't work to the advantage of a lawyer who is trying to evoke a sensitive reaction. More important than that bit of costuming, though, was the fact that I learned you never try to tell a jury what to do. No more do I point my finger and say it is their duty to find my way. I moved to the use of open gestures with the hope of soliciting jurors to come my way in a much less confrontational manner.

In the summer of 1980, the Vermont Trappers Association planned to host a national meeting for trappers from all over the country. It was planned for August at the fair grounds in Rutland. Trappers and their families, totaling almost ten thousand in number, were expected to arrive, stay in campers or in local motels, and meet to discuss fur trapping. There was to be an exhibition of suppliers to the industry and, all-in-all, it promised to be a festive occasion. The leadership of the Vermont Trappers Association was concerned the event might be big enough to attract animal rights protestors, and in an abundance of caution, they retained me to be available to represent them should any problems arise during the event. The meeting went off without any problems whatsoever, and the trappers returned to their homes around the country, looking forward to the upcoming trapping season.

Differing costumes were never more apparent than when, early the next spring, I was invited to speak to the Annual Vermont Trappers Association Meeting. I figured the appropriate costume for this meeting for me was my best three-piece suit, as I expected the assembled trappers wanted their lawyer to look like a lawyer and not a trapper. I could talk trapping with them comfortably, but I wanted them to feel confident that if they needed legal help, they were getting a real lawyer and not a trapper as their counsel.

While trapping in Vermont no longer ranks as a leading industry, the annual harvest of beaver, mink, muskrat, otter, and raccoon amounts to more than one million dollars of outside monies injected into the state's economy. In my short presentation, I reviewed the plans made for hosting the national meeting and, thankfully, my minimal role in the actual event, as nothing had happened which required legal services. I then discussed some pending legislation and sat down to polite applause.

The man who spoke after me was dressed in a neat sports jacket and an open shirt, and as he rose to speak to the assemblage of trappers dressed in checked woolen shirts and Johnson woolen pants held up by large galluses, I wondered who he was, and it didn't take me long to find out.

He spoke with a heavy French-Canadian accent and said, "I not kid you, I come here to buy your furs. I work for a company, a good company, an old company, the Hudson Bay Company." He then went on to discuss the probable prices for furs that year, indicating there was a greater demand for long-hair furs than short-hair furs. He told them that he had brought a Hudson Bay blanket to donate for the auction to be held later that day, to help raise monies for the Association. The applause he received was a great deal more enthusiastic than my reception had been.

I can remember thinking to myself about the continuum of history. Here in the 1980s, the Hudson Bay Company, which had been founded in 1648 and controlled the fur trade through the northern United States and Canada during the frontier days, was still hustling furs and trading blankets with a group dressed not much differently from the way their ancestors dressed in the early days of the fur trade.

I bought the Hudson Bay blanket at the auction and have it to this day.

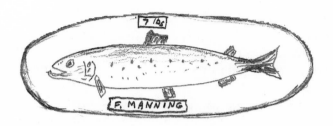

11.

FISH STORIES

Rochester is a typical picturesque Vermont town. It is a small community snuggled in the hills, and in winter it gets more than its fair share of snow and in summer less than its fair share of long, sunny days. The village green, in the center of town, is surrounded by stately old houses, among them on its south side, a large white building that in the 1960s housed the Rochester Inn. Here was a watering hole for the thirsty inhabitants of the beautiful Route 100 valley. Proudly displayed over the bar was a stuffed seven-pound brown trout, which beauty was a major subject of discussion among those who chose to wet their whistle at this taproom. It was the largest brown trout ever caught in the nearby upstream section of the White River. A brass plaque, attached to the board on which the fish was mounted, bore the name of the successful fisherman, Fred Manning. It also set forth the weight and length of the trout, and the date of its demise.

For most of the natives of the area surrounding Rochester, hunting and fishing are the major recreational activities. The bar at the inn was never better patronized than during deer season. The only comparable time, from a business standpoint, was when the trout

95

season opened. No large buck, no large trout, is ever killed or caught just once. The stories of the hunt and the catch are told and retold, sometimes with slight changes and exaggerations. Thus, this stuffed brown trout became not only the focal point of the story of how it was caught, but also the catalyst for many other fishing stories of successes achieved far from the upper reaches of the White River.

The White River starts on the eastern slopes of the Green Mountains, its waters lining the west side of the Route 100 valley above Rochester, and then flowing down the valley along Route 100 until they approach Stockbridge, where they veer on an eastward course, finally emptying into the Connecticut River. About ten miles southeast of Rochester, the United States Government has built and maintains an Atlantic salmon hatchery. Each year now there are reports of several hundred Atlantic salmon which have started at the hatchery and made their great odyssey through the Atlantic Ocean to the shores of Greenland, returning to the White River two years later as mature fish. While success in returning the White River into the great salmon fishery it was in pre-colonial times is a long way off, every local fisherperson dreams about the excitement of hooking a large fish in the upper rapids or deep pools of the White River. At the time of the capture of the brown trout that ended up stuffed and displayed above the bar at the Rochester Inn, there was no salmon run, and this fish was the embodiment of every stream fisherperson's great fantasy.

Every law student hears of, but seldom learns much about, the ancient writs of "replevin" and "detinue." I never learned much about detinue, but replevin always had a certain amount of fascination for me. In a writ of replevin, a claim is made that someone else is holding personal property that belongs to the plaintiff, and the plaintiff signs an affidavit to that effect. Armed with this affidavit and a bond to protect the potential defendant should the plaintiff be proven wrong, the court issues papers commanding the sheriff to go take into possession the article of personal property sought by the replevor.

One day, Fred Manning walked into my office in Middlebury and told this story: Several years earlier he had been fishing in a section of the White River when a fish struck his fly like no fish had ever hit his fly before. After a long struggle with the fish, taking the better part of an hour, he was finally able to beach it on the gravel banks of the stream, one hundred yards down from where he had originally hooked it. It was a magnificent fish, and like most fishermen, he couldn't wait to brag about it. He promptly got into his pickup truck and made his way to the Rochester Inn, where he proudly displayed the trout, with the suggestion that it would be perfectly appropriate for anyone to buy him a beer to celebrate his great catch. After several beers, someone suggested that the fish was such a beauty, it would be a shame to simply eat it and forget about it, but rather, it should be mounted so that future fishers on the White River would know what that river could actually produce.

An Aside

Fred, when he wasn't fishing, was a dogger at Eaton's Lumber Mill. A dogger got the logs into position manually for the sawyer. This was before the automatic log carriage came out, and riding the logs into position was a hard and dirty job. To keep production up, Eaton offered a bonus based on the quantity of lumber sawed. Fred worked hard to make his bonus, but always referred to his bonus as the number of extra beers he had earned and not as extra dollars.

Fred had one problem, which was a rather common one in the valley in those days, and that was that he had no money with which to pay a taxidermist. After a few more beers, the owner of the Rochester Inn suggested a solution. He would advance the monies for the stuffing of the fish and it would be proudly displayed over the bar at the Rochester Inn. This was almost acceptable to Fred, but he indicated that it was his fish, and if it were to be mounted, he might someday want to have it in his home. The proprietor quickly clinched the deal by saying that at any time Fred got the money to reimburse him for the cost of the mounting of the fish, he could have it back and take it home. This bargain was sealed with another round of drinks all the way around and the fish was taken, frozen, and the next day sent to Vermont's best taxidermist, Philip Brooks, up in Glover.

The proprietor kept his word and paid for the mounting. In due time the fish, together with its small brass plaque, was returned to the Rochester Inn, where it was placed in a prominent spot above the bar. And there it stayed for several years. During this period the fish and its conqueror received a certain amount of local notoriety, although no one was ever to glean from Fred exactly which pool on the White River had been the one in which he had hooked the fish.

Shortly before he came to see me, he had some falling out with the locals at the Rochester Inn and decided it was time to retrieve his fish. He managed to get together a sum of money equal to what the proprietor had paid the taxidermist, and brought it into the bar to give him. He laid the money on the bar, claiming his right to take the stuffed brown trout home with him. This did not sit well with the owner, who had come to realize that, silly as it may have seemed, he had become fond of the stuffed trout. He recognized that, as a decoration for his bar, it had become a talking point and its removal might result in a loss of some business. He refused Manning's money and said that while a deal had been made some years before, he was no longer prepared to turn the fish over to its conqueror merely because of the repayment of a sum that he had put out some years ago. Manning walked out of the bar, and that's when he came to see me.

While I had often fantasized about catching a trout of this size, I had never come close to doing so, either in the White River or in any other Vermont stream. I had a certain empathy for his position and I agreed to bring what was my first, and only, writ of replevin. We offered the sum we believed due, and when the owner refused it, we sent the sheriff, armed with a writ and with a bond, to take down the fish from the Rochester Inn bar. The writ was returnable to the Windsor Superior Court in Woodstock.

Fortunately, shortly after the writ was served and the fish taken into possession by Sheriff Al Chandler, common sense prevailed and the reluctant proprietor adhered to the original agreement.

While Fred was happy, I am not sure the community was well served by having this beautiful trophy trout moved from the bar at the Inn to Fred's small living room.

Unfortunately, the same problem that had plagued Fred initially in not being able to stuff his own trout, plagued him still, and he was unable to pay his attorney's fees. I chalked the lack of payment up to experience and figured that not every lawyer had the opportunity to replevy a stuffed brown trout. Before writing off my fees completely, I stopped by his house one day late in the afternoon as I was returning from court on the east side of the state. I had packed my fish pole and waders in the car, and I had a couple of hours before sunset when I hoped to try my luck in the White River. I asked Fred for some advice as to where and how to fish the river, and more specifically requested him to tell me how to get to the pool where he had hooked the seven pounder. He was reluctant at first, but when I promised not to disclose the location, and after I reminded him that if it were not for my intervention, the stuffed trout would still be sitting over the bar at the Rochester Inn, he gave me specific instructions on how to get to a particular stretch of the River and how to fish it. I followed his instructions to a tee, and while I did get several nice brown trout that evening, none of them came close to approaching the big one. Whether or not he actually steered me to the exact location is unimportant, because I could now write off his legal fees with my head held high as the fees having been satisfied in kind by an important fishing tip. As far as I knew then and know to this day, that fee did not require being reported to the IRS.

Richard Spooner was a disabled Vietnam veteran; he was paralyzed from the waist down. Dick was nevertheless an avid hunter and fisherperson. He even organized veterans' groups throughout New England to set up special facilities for disabled people to participate in the great outdoors. His only child was a twelve-year-old daughter named Carrie who liked to accompany her father on his fishing expeditions. One time in the summer of 1992, both of them entered the Lake Champlain Fishing Derby. To enter it you paid a fee and hoped to catch a fish that would qualify you for some very substantial prizes. There was a prize for the largest of each species and also a prize for the fish which, on a percentage basis, came closest to being a world record for that species. The tournament encouraged the participants to keep the fish alive in a tank so they could be weighed, measured, and then returned to the lake.

Among the species that can be found in the south lake are the Ling and the Bowfin. Both of these fish are bottom feeders which trace back to prehistoric times. Dick and Carrie were fishing in the south lake when Carrie tied into a fish weighing 7 pounds. They were unsure of the exact species, so they put it in their tank and brought it into the weighing-in station. As Carrie carried the fish to the weighing station, several locals watching the weighing in ceremonies chimed in that she had caught one hell of a Ling. The biologist in attendance then identified the fish as a Ling, weighed it carefully, took its measurements, and returned it to Carrie. She released it back into Lake

Champlain. When the measurements of the fish and the species were reported to the Derby's central committee, it became clear that this was a truly exceptional Ling, possibly a world record, and certainly the grand-prize catch of the tournament. However, the organizers of the event had not seen the fish, and they suspected that it was not a Ling but a Bowfin. They conducted an investigation which included talking to the biologist to get his description of the fish. They overruled the attending biologist and concluded that it was a Bowfin of ordinary size which would result in no prize to Carrie. They notified Carrie that her entry was disqualified based upon this investigation. Richard and Carrie came in to see me, showed me the receipt they had, which had been prepared by the Derby's very own biologist that indicated the fish was a Ling. They pointed out that they had returned the live fish to the lake and had only the receipt for proof of the species. If it was a Ling, Carrie was entitled to prizes in excess of $10,000. Attempts to deal with the Lake Champlain Fishing Derby Committee were to no avail. Suit was brought in the Addison Superior Court against the organization, with Dick Spooner acting as the guardian of his daughter. Dick Affolter, a lawyer from Burlington, made his appearance on behalf of the Lake Champlain Fishing Derby Committee. He informed me he had been instructed to defend the case and that the defense was being provided by the Derby's insurance carrier, Lloyds of London.

The Fourth Estate loved this story. Carrie was interviewed on local television and she told how she had caught the fish, brought it to the check-in station, had it weighed, and gone back jubilant because she was going to receive a large cash prize which she could save toward her college education. The fact that Carrie's father was a disabled veteran who had managed to get to the boat in a wheelchair to take his daughter fishing didn't diminish media attention.

The publicity soon died down and the case remained on the docket of the Addison Superior Court for some period of time. Eventually, the insurance carrier gave Dick Affolter the authority to settle the case but on condition that the sum remain confidential. While the monies offered were less than what the full prize would have been, given the risks of litigation, Carrie and Dick decided to take the settlement. It still amounted to a lot of dollars per pound for a fish that is probably still swimming around in the bottom of Lake Champlain.

Fisherpersons are a different sort of people, and one of the most different was Francis O'Brien.

One day Francis, Pop Stearns, Bill Rule and I were up in the Northeast Kingdom fishing for lake trout. We were fishing Long Pond which was a highly productive trout lake with lots of lakers in the two-to-three pound class. This was before the days of fish finders, outriggers, and the like, and in order to get down to the bottom, you used wire line. Bill and I each had our own outfit, but Francis had borrowed one from a friend of his in Panton by the name of Sullivan. The borrowed outfit had a single strand copper line. The trouble with a single strand line is if it gets a kink in it and a fish pulls on it, the line will break at the kink. It requires very careful handling. Care of a fishing line, and especially wire line, was not one of Francis's talents.

Pop Stearns and I were trolling the lake in one boat, and Bill and Francis were in the other. Bill was at the motor. We were trolling past a point where there was a fisherman on shore who had cast way out in the lake and was letting his bait lie on the bottom hoping a feeding trout would come along. Francis hooked the line of the man on shore, and pretty soon the two of them were pulling at each other, each thinking they had a hell of a fish. By the time they realized that it wasn't a fish, the guy on shore was giving Francis holy hell for having trolled across his line. That didn't bother Francis at all. He just pulled in his heavy copper line, took out his jackknife, and cut the shore fisherman's line. Rant and rave as he did, the fisherman with the cut line had no access to Francis, who in response to the threats coming from shore, simply responded "sue me" and kept on fishing.

Getting Francis to concentrate was sometimes difficult to do. During the course of that same day Francis's lure kept getting caught on the bottom, resulting in losses of chunks of line as it broke off at various kinks that had been ignored by Francis in his seemingly constant pattern of getting it tangled. Finally, at one point, after hitting a snag on the bottom, his line once again broke, leaving his spoon and a large portion of the remaining line on the bottom. He pulled in the rest of the line hand-over-hand, and ended up with a bird's nest of wire cradled in the bottom of the boat. Our boat was fairly close, and Pop Stearns and I watched this whole charade. With his line in a complete tangle, Francis decided to give up fishing for the day. Bill started their motor, intending to troll his line and head back towards the landing spot. Francis stood up in the boat and said, "That's the last we will ever see of that son-of-a-bitch," and he took the bird's nest of wire and threw it overboard. In about five seconds we could hear the motor on their boat grind to a halt. Somehow Francis had managed to throw the wire into the water in such a way that it got caught by the propeller and completely wound itself around it, stopping the motor cold. Bill patiently took the motor off the back of the boat, took off the prop, unwound the wire, and repaired the damage that had been done. The motor then made it back to the back of the boat and the boat to the shore. I never did find out how Francis explained the loss of all the line to Mr. Sullivan.

12.
HORSES

Every once in a while you realize you've blown a chance to say something really significant, to make you look like a hero. Most times you think of exactly the right thing to say twenty-four hours after you have had the opportunity to say it. I remember an occasion when I wanted to make a comment but was too timid, and I have always regretted not speaking up. It was early in the 1980s at a meeting of the American Law Institute. ALI is a group of self-important, self-selected lawyers, mostly white and male. At its inception in 1923 there was a belief that certain underlying principles of law could be reduced to simple rules and these rules would be useful in curing the intellectual ills of the legal system. Despite the institute's self-selected pomposity, it has served the legal profession well. Among its projects are the so-called "Restatements of the Law." These are compilations of principles, commentary, and illustrations. They try to strike a balance between the way the law actually is, as shown in the precedents of court decisions, and the way the ALI thinks it should be.

The annual meeting of the institute is held each May, usually in Washington, D.C. in the grand ballroom of the landmark Mayflower

Hotel. The members of the institute are invited to participate in discussions concerning the drafts of the Restatements. The sessions are led by the reporter who has been the principal draftsperson in preparing the Restatements.

On one occasion, E. Allan Farnsworth, a professor at Columbia University Law School, who exemplifies the image of stiffness and pomposity, was leading a discussion on a revision of the "Restatement of Contracts." He indicated that, as the reporter for the revision, he was going to do away with a whole series of illustrations that had become an important part of the first Restatement, because those illustrations used horses as the commodity of the transaction and horses were no longer relevant.

This is where I missed my chance. I wanted to take the microphone and say, "Horses may not be relevant to you at Columbia Law School, Professor Farnsworth, but we country lawyers find an important part of our practice revolves around horses. Just last week I dealt with four cases involving horses: in the first, my client riding a motorcycle hit a horse; in the second, a client sold a horse that was supposedly barren, but was in fact pregnant; the third case involved a dissolution of a race-horse partnership; and in the fourth, my clients' horses were getting out of the pasture and trampling a neighbor's garden." Alas, my timidity prevented me from saying anything, and I have ever since regretted the missed opportunity to provoke a guffaw in the institute and take a little out of Farnsworth's pomposity.

During the nineteenth century, there was a great deal of litigation over horses. Horses were a major source of power to run machinery and, even more important, provided localized transportation. Disputes often went all the way to the Vermont Supreme Court involving lawsuits over horses and are recorded in the Vermont Reports. The surprising thing is that horses are still an important part of the agricultural community and can still be the grist for litigation.

Percy Davis is one of the all-time great trainers of harness horses at Saratoga Raceway. He's known as "The Wizard of Trotters." Percy never moved far from Saratoga, but many times trainers and owners who had problem trotters would send them to Saratoga for Percy's ability to straighten them out and get them back to the races. On one occasion, a lawyer from Brooklyn, New York, owned a horse named High Basis. A son of the great sire, Rodney, High Basis had tremendous potential. Unfortunately, he had been injured early in his racing career and his legs no longer could take the strain of top-class racing. The owner sent him up to Percy, who worked with him for eight weeks, and then informed the owner that High Basis's legs were so bad that he did not think he could ever return to the major tracks as a top competitor. The owner, who had already incurred a couple of months of training bills, asked Percy if he would be willing to take the horse in payment for the bills. Percy indicated he would. The bills were wiped out, and High Basis was registered to Percy.

Over the next several months, Percy worked hard on the horse's legs, using all the tricks of his trade. Even though the horse was bred to be a trotter, having the conventional diagonal gate, Percy converted it to be a pacer, as that gait, in which the legs on the same side move forward at the same time, is easier on a horse's legs. Time went on, and Percy entered the horse in a qualifying race, a race with no purse but which is required in order to make sure the horse is fit to race and to give bettors at pari-mutuel tracks at least one recent past-performance line to look at when trying to handicap that horse. High Basis qualified and was entered into a two- thousand-dollar claiming race, one that allows any horseperson to buy the horse by depositing the amount of the claiming price with the race secretary before the race. Title to the horse transfers to the new owner when the word "go" is given to start the race. The old owner keeps the purse and the new owner takes possession of the horse and its halter at the end of the race. High Basis won his race, and received fifty percent of the one-thousand-dollar purse. Someone liked the way he paced and offered to buy him from Percy for the claiming price of two thousand dollars. Percy sold the horse. However, under the new owner's training regime, the horse's legs did not stand up, and he soon went lame without any further success at the track. The purchaser came to Percy and asked if he would be willing to buy the horse back, albeit at a substantial discount from the two-thousand-dollar figure. Percy agreed, and once again with the horse back in his care, he started working his magic by using his special potions on the horse's legs. After several months High Basis was again fit to race. Percy qualified the horse and then entered him in another two-thousand-dollar claiming race. High Basis produced another win. This prompted a new buyer, and High Basis had another owner.

The new owner attempted to race the horse, and, in its second start, the horse once again went lame. The second purchaser came back to Percy and Percy bought the horse back, again at a discount from what he had sold it for.

Percy gave the horse several months off and then carefully worked to bring him back to racing condition. This time his magic seemed to stick and, keeping the horse, Percy raced him regularly in low-priced claiming races. In October of 1974, I had the pleasure to drive him and to bring him into the winner's circle at Saratoga. High Basis chalked up nine wins, five places, and four shows in twenty-six starts that year. At the awards banquet he was designated the claimer of the year at Saratoga Raceway.

Meanwhile, back in Brooklyn, the original owner, reading the weekly magazine, the *Harness Horse*, which printed the results of all the races, saw how successful High Basis had been. He decided either he had been had by Percy or, at least, that he might be able to get some money out of him. He brought suit in Kings County Court in Brooklyn, claiming that Percy had committed fraud in the purchase of the horse. He claimed Percy had told him this horse would never race again, at a time when Percy had superior knowledge and knew that the horse, with proper care, would once again be a great race horse. Percy's defense was that he had never said the horse wouldn't race again. He had said the horse would never be able to compete at the high level of the New York City racing scene. This was true, as High Basis under Percy's careful eye always raced in low-priced claiming races.

The time came for the trial and I picked Percy up at Saratoga at about 3:00 a.m. for the drive to New York City and a 9:30 trial. We were to meet our New York counsel, Stuart Frum, an old friend and a horseman from Westport, New York, at the court in Brooklyn where the trial was scheduled. I remember getting caught in New York City traffic from the Tappan Zee Bridge south and wondering if I was ever going to get to Brooklyn. I drove down East River Drive, crossed the Brooklyn Bridge, parked the car, and we arrived at the court at exactly 9:28 a.m.

Percy was brought up in Massena, New York. With limited exposure outside of upstate New York, he was a bit disconcerted when he realized we were in a section of Brooklyn populated by Hasidic Jews with their black hats, beards, and curls. This was a long way from the back stretch of a racetrack where Percy was at home and where he felt in control.

Stuart Frum and I were called into the judge's chambers along with opposing counsel to see if there was any possibility of a settlement. When it appeared the case would have to be tried, the court gave us a few minutes to get ready before calling us into the courtroom to hear the evidence.

I had told Percy to wear his Sunday best for trial, and he was dressed in the suit he had gotten married in some fifteen years earlier. Its lapels were about one inch wide, and, as Percy had matured through the arms and shoulders, it came nowhere near to closure in front. It looked almost like a gray cape with arms. Percy had very powerful arms, which in part came from driving horses that sometimes take the bit in their teeth and try to run away with the driver. He looked spectacular as he was called to the stand. To put him in perspective: my wife named the first ram she introduced to her flock of sheep "Percy."

The plaintiff's lawyer called Percy to the stand as his first witness. Percy, both because he was uncomfortable in the Brooklyn court-room, and because of his natural gait, approached the stand with a sort of cowboy swagger, rolling from one side to the other as he walked to the witness chair. I still recall the look on the face of the court reporter as Percy took the stand. She was a rather buxom woman and she looked Percy over from top to bottom. If men are accused of undressing women with their eyes, this was the flip side of that accusation. She smiled broadly as he took the stand. The court officer, a black man, was clearly intrigued with the appearance of what was obviously a country man and not a native Brooklynite.

After a few preliminary questions, the plaintiff's lawyer got down to the brass tacks of his case. He asked a long and convoluted question while Percy listened carefully. The question went something like this. "Now, Mr. Davis, if I understand this matter, you got this horse and you worked on this horse, and this horse won a race for you, and you sold the horse. The horse then went lame and you bought the horse back. You again worked on the horse and it won another race, and you sold it and then it went lame again. Why did you buy the horse back the second time if it was lame?" Percy, without so much as a blink, gave the most straightforward and effective answer I have ever heard delivered in a courtroom. "I felt sorry for the horse." The court reporter, the bailiff, and even the judge, all responded with broad grins, giving proof of Percy's credibility.

In trying to recover, the plaintiff's lawyer took another tack. He questioned Percy about driving a horse that had gone lame on two previous occasions, and asked why he should take the risk of driving a horse so prone to lameness. Percy looked at him and said, "That's not the way it is," and then started to explain to him about how to work on the legs of a race horse. Shortly thereafter, plaintiff's counsel abandoned his examination of Percy Davis.

On my examination of Percy, he went on to tell his story about what was said at the time of the purchase of the horse, about the vagaries of horse lameness, and how he had always raced the horse at a level where it would not be pushed to the ultimate, thereby decreasing its risk of injury. At the close of the evidence, the court gave its decision from the bench. Percy was seated in the back of the courtroom. The court made its findings that no fraud had been committed and that the plaintiff was to take nothing by his lawsuit. As soon as the court recessed, I stepped toward the back of the courtroom and said to Percy, "We won." Percy looked at me and said, "I thought the judge was saying some things that were pretty good."

We got back in our car and left Brooklyn for the trip to Saratoga Raceway. Stu Frum was with us and as he was driving, Percy and I decided to celebrate. Stu's father had a liquor store in Yonkers, and Percy bought a bottle of a chocolate mint liqueur and I bought a bottle of brandy. Percy was not much of a drinker, but that chocolate mint flavored liqueur tasted awfully good to him. When we arrived at the track, Percy and I were both well into our cups. It was the only time in more than thirty years of racing at Saratoga that Percy Davis ever had dinner at the Club House at Saratoga Raceway. He couldn't see the horses on the track. He later reported that it took him four days to get over the hangover. As for High Basis, he was retired two years later to stud in Iowa.

On another occasion I had a chance to represent a wonderful old Vermonter, Floyd Partridge, who lived near Springfield. He loved harness racing and was a good horseperson. A dispute arose involving a horse he had leased for racing purposes. The horse had been having a good season at Hinsdale Raceway in New Hampshire, just across the Connecticut River from the Vermont town of Brattleboro. The owner decided he wanted the horse back. The case made its way to trial at the Windsor County Courthouse in Woodstock, another of Vermont's beautiful old courthouses, sitting on the town green, just north of the Woodstock Inn. The old Woodstock Inn, a four-story wooden building, was torn down in the mid-1960s and replaced by an imposing Rockefeller resort hotel. In 1961, nearly half of the entire Vermont Bar gathered on the wooden benches in the back of the second floor courtroom of the Windsor County Courthouse for a special session of the U.S. Court of Appeals for the Second Circuit. More than one hundred members of the bar were sworn in, the only ceremonial session ever held just for that purpose in Vermont. This courthouse has the added distinction of being the only courthouse in the state to preserve the tradition of ringing the courthouse bell to announce to the community that a jury has reached a verdict.

The Honorable William Larrow was presiding in Floyd Partridge's case. Larrow, a graduate of Harvard Law School, was an extremely bright lawyer with a keen sense of humor. In this particular case, my opponent's attorney had identified a picture of the horse in question, taken in the winner's circle at Hinsdale Raceway. When counsel offered it as an exhibit, Larrow, knowing of my participation in the sport, turned to him and said, "Would you please show that exhibit to Mr. Langrock? He hasn't seen many winners." Fortunately, after a half day of trial we were able to settle the case.

In the fall of 1966 I acquired my first harness horse. In early 1967 I bought my second harness horse, a horse called Caroline's Glow. At that time, there was a winter harness meet at Green Mountain Park in Pownal in the southern part of the state. The thoroughbreds ran there in the summer, and they had a harness meet running from late fall to the spring, keeping racing going on a year-round basis. In March, Carolyn's Glow was entered in a race, the first in which I would be the owner of a horse that was actually racing, and I was quite excited about it. This was long before I qualified as a trainer and driver myself and my knowledge of what was going to happen was somewhat incomplete. I knew one thing for sure, my wife and I were going to watch the race. Francis O'Brien, his wife Madeleine, and Bill and Charmaine Rule joined us in our excursion to Pownal. We found a motel so that we would not have to drive all the way home after the races. Caroline's Glow was in the fourth race, and by the time the moment came around, we had finished an early dinner in the club house, and were at the rail of the track. I had made a small wager on the horse, and I suggested to my compatriots that they do the same. The track at Green Mountain Park was five-eighths of a mile around, with the starting line on the back side. The horses came around counterclockwise in front of the grandstand and made another complete circle before finishing in front of the grandstand. When the mobile starting gate pulled away from the field at the start of the race, Caroline's Glow quickly maneuvered herself into last place. She stayed there for the entire race and I am not sure she's ever reached the finish line to this date. I had learned my first lesson in horse racing: your horse doesn't always win.

As I was trying to come up with a rationalization for my horse's failure to even make a respectable showing, Francis sidled up to me and showed me a pari-mutuel ticket he had purchased on the winning horse. The horse was a second favorite and paid eight dollars to win. I looked at Francis, dismayed at his lack of loyalty to my horse, and asked, "How did you ever pick out that horse?" He made a comment about talking to some fellows at a garage that morning and their giving him a tip on the horse. I was quite upset. Francis had never mentioned anything about that in our trip to the track. At every opportunity that evening, as we watched the rest of the races and then returned to our motel, he kept poking at me about how he had picked the winner and how my horse had performed rather badly. He continued to pick at me about my horse well into the next morning's breakfast when, finally, he took pity and confessed that he had planned the whole thing by buying a two-dollar ticket on each of the eight horses in the race. He always maintained it was well worth his eight-dollar net loss just to see the expression on my face when he held out that winning ticket.

Most lawyers know the case from the Michigan Supreme Court involving "The Rose of Aberlone." Rose was a polled Angus cow believed to be barren that had been sold as a cull to be used for beef rather than as a brood cow. Actually, she was pregnant, and the price paid for her as a cull was substantially less than what would have been paid had the buyer known she was fertile, carrying a calf. The case involved a mutual mistake of fact between the buyer and the seller, and the question before the court was whether, based upon that mutual mistake, there should be a recision or a voiding of the original contract, putting the parties back where they were before the sale had been made.

One day a horse breeder from Cornwall by the name of Lyons walked into my office and said he had sold a mare, believing she was not in foal. It turned out she was in foal, and the person who bought her was now asking him to sign the breeding certificate so the horse could be registered with the American Morgan Horse Association. My client was angry, as the purchaser was a veterinarian, and the same veterinarian who had pronounced that the mare was not carrying a foal. I remembered the case involving "The Rose of Aberlone," but I couldn't remember which way the court had decided. I went rummaging through my old contract books from law school and finally located the case, which held that their mutual mistake was a sufficient reason for a court to order a recision. We were able to negotiate an advantageous settlement.

Any large animal, like a horse or a cow, that breaks out of its pasture and gets onto a road, is a potential menace to drivers. When somebody is injured, or a vehicle is badly damaged by an animal that has escaped from the pasture, there is always the question of whether the owner of the pasture has been negligent in maintaining the fence and gates which failed to contain the animal.

One of my clients boarded a horse for a friend. The horse got through the fence and was struck by an automobile, killing the horse and damaging the vehicle. The client was getting hit from both directions, by the owner of the horse and by the owner of the vehicle. The client, when asked about the fence, replied that it was a barbed-wire fence and was kept in good condition. She said she had just one problem. There was a moose in the area and on two previous occasions the moose had simply walked through the fence, ignoring the barbed wire and opening it up so any animal in the pasture could get out. Our defense to the claims of the owner of the horse and the driver of the car was that it was an act of God, or, at least, it was the moose's fault and not my client's negligence that allowed the horse to get into the road. Fortunately, the owner of the car had collision coverage. The friend who had boarded the horse, recognizing there was little that my client could have done, did not pursue her claim. As moose are immune from suit in Vermont, it was a case resolved without a court proceeding and without anybody having to pay any money on a liability claim.

John and Lucy Button live on a mountain farm, just north of Tunbridge, Vermont. John's father, Glen, has been a horseperson all of his life. Glen's interest in horses runs to working teams, and John and Lucy's interest in horses runs to standardbreds, or harness racehorses. Over the years, with the increasing costs of producing milk and declining milk prices, the mountain farms in Tunbridge became less attractive, from an operational standpoint, as dairy farms. The Buttons switched from an operating dairy to raising dairy replacement heifers, young females which are raised from shortly after birth until such time as they are bred and ready to calf. Calving allows the young cow to start producing milk and become a part of a milking-dairy herd.

There is nothing like the Tunbridge World's Fair. The fairgrounds are set on a small piece of flat land located along the First Branch of the White River that runs through the village of Tunbridge. The narrow half-mile-long race track is a challenge to negotiate. Coming down the stretch, the track widens to allow three horses to go side-by-side. Thus, only three horses can line up in the first tier behind the starting car, and any additional horses have to line up in a second tier behind the first three horses. The far side of the track narrows even further, allowing horses to go only two wide; that is, two side-by-side. If a horse tries to go three wide, someone is liable to end up in the river. The purses for racing at the fair are small, but the camaraderie and the fact that racing has continued over the same track for more than a hundred years make it a very special place.

One of the traditional events at Tunbridge each year is the special race for fourteen-year-old horses. Under the Rules of the United States Trotting Association, horses are allowed to race only through their fourteenth year. Tunbridge, coming in the month of September, draws some wonderful old racehorses for their final race. Each horse in the race receives a trophy. While the competition in the fourteen-year-old race may be less than in the other races, the emotions run high for the drivers, many of whom are racing a horse they have raised from birth, continued to own and race at fairs and racetracks, and are finally retiring at the age of fourteen.

I can remember driving Dick Lane, a trotter, in 1973 in his last race. We had won the first heat, but as we reached the stretch in the second heat, it looked as if we were going to be beat. As I tapped him with the whip, it seemed as if he recognized the significance of the race, and he put on a burst of speed to win by a head over Rhapsody in Blue, with Pop Song and Hardy's Pudding close behind. One week later he was participating under saddle at the Addison County Field Days grounds in a trail class at a local horse show. The judge at the horse show was about to award him reserve champion; he was truly handsome at a trot. When all the horses were lined up side by side in the center of the ring, the judge asked each of the horses to back up. This was one thing Dick Lane had never learned at the track and his failure to do so cost him his ribbon.

For many years John and Lucy Button kept several racehorses on the fairgrounds at Tunbridge, training them, for the most part, for seasonal racing at the fairs around the states of Vermont, New Hampshire, and New York, but especially for the Tunbridge Fair itself. As an outgrowth of their interest in racing, John and Lucy occasionally raised foals on their Tunbridge farm. On one occasion they had a fine old mare which had been bred to one of their own studs. The offspring was probably not destined to become a winner of the Hambletonian, or even to become a racehorse on a major track. It, however, was destined to be raised with loving care, and would surely have been part of the Buttons' racing stable. Mares, usually bred in the spring, have an eleven-month gestation period and are expected to foal the following spring. Thus, in November, one would find the mare out in pasture grazing at what grass is left, its feed being supplemented by hay and grain.

One of the other aspects of the Buttons' hill farm in Tunbridge is that it lies in a heavily wooded area where there is awfully good deer hunting. Some deer hunters are more competent than others, and some are more careful than others. In the fall of 1981, a hunter happened to mistake the Buttons' broodmare for a deer, and dropped it in its tracks with a well-placed rifle shot. The Buttons were upset and came to see me about what they could do. I suggested that they had a good legal claim for the value of the horse, and I would be happy to undertake the case on their behalf.

The first thing I did was to research the breeding of the mare that had been killed. The United States Trotting Association each year produces a book entitled *Sires and Dams.* That book contains a listing of all active broodmares and stallions. Under each mare there is a listing of the offspring that mare has produced and certain essential information about each of the offspring, including the fastest time the horse ever went for one mile on a racetrack and its money winnings.

With most every racehorse, if you research its pedigree, you will find in very close generations some outstanding sires. This is because the stallion can cover about fifty mares a year naturally, or as many as two hundred by the use of artificial insemination, and, therefore, only the best, fastest, and most successful stallions are used for stud purposes. No standardbred is very far in pedigree from a world champion.

I collected all this information and wrote a demand letter to the homeowner's insurance company that insured the man who had shot the horse. I was able to show not only her breeding back to many successful horses but that close relatives of the mare had been exceptionally successful, having won hundreds of thousands of dollars in purses. This was not really that difficult, as most any standardbred mare could produce a similarly attractive pedigree. I went on to explain in my demand letter the circumstances of the horse being killed, and I made what I claimed to be a modest demand of five thousand dollars to settle the case. A week later, I got a letter back from the insurance company, in which they enclosed a general release and a check for the full five thousand dollar demand. It is not every day an insurance company meets your initial demand. I think, actually, in this case, they were quite wise to do so. However, it did make me wonder whether or not I had asked for enough in the first place.

My fears in this regard were removed when I talked to my clients about the settlement and gave them their share of the proceeds, after deducting legal fees. John looked at me and said, "I've got another mare. Do you think I should invite this fella back for deer hunting next year?"

Two diverse and wonderful persons came into open conflict on the political scene. One was Richard Blum, a graduate of Brooklyn Law School, and the lawyer selected to be the second director of Legal Aid in Vermont. Richard is, and always has been, a serious and competent advocate for the little people of the world. He also has a wonderful sense of humor, and while sometimes it may be a little off-beat, he has the capacity to laugh at himself.

AN ASIDE

I learned to appreciate Richard when I was hospitalized with an eye injury in 1955. Each evening at the hospital he would sneak in after visiting hours and tell me stories of the day's doings in the courts and legal world. I learned from him how to minister to a sick or injured person by entertaining and not dwelling on the sickness or the injury itself.

The other person involved was Dean Davis, who was governor of Vermont from 1969 through 1973. Davis had been a state's attorney, and then a superior judge, and going on to become president of National Life Insurance Company. After stepping down as president of National Life, he was drafted by the conservative wing of the Vermont Republican Party to run against Jim Oakes, a Republican moderate, in the gubernatorial primary in 1968, which Davis won. Dean Davis was a gentleman, a quality lawyer, and he represented the opposite extreme of the political spectrum from Richard Blum.

When a controversy broke out between them concerning Legal Aid's budget, it made its way into the papers, and, as often happens, the journalists turned what had been a political and philosophical disagreement into a personal war.

Governor Davis was known throughout the state as a strong admirer of the Morgan horse. He loved to ride and would be seen in many parades throughout the state astride his Morgan. His love for horses was a recognized attribute, virtually a trademark of his governorship.

One day I received a call from Richard, who, knowing I had some horse connections, asked me if I knew where he could buy a Morgan horse cheap. I asked him some questions about what kind of horse he wanted and what he wanted it for, and he said there were only two requirements, one that it be a Morgan, and the other that it be cheap. On further questioning as to why he wanted to buy a horse with only those two qualifications, he said he was so pissed off at the governor that he wanted to have a big party and barbeque the horse in honor of the governor. I think he was half serious. Fortunately for all concerned, the plan never came to fruition, but the story of his proposed barbeque spread throughout the state.

13.
FARMING'S VICISSITUDES

I never knew where Francis O'Brien came from. I first ran into him in 1960 when I was running for State's Attorney of Addison County. He was already a local legend by that time. He had recently met a charming young widow named Madeleine Hoffnagle, and had totally and completely fallen in love. Madeleine, likewise, seemed to be very much in love with Francis and enjoyed the never-ending succession of surprises he brought to their marriage.

Francis, as a young man, operated a meat cart, peddling meat from house to house around Middlebury. He also bought and sold livestock. He took on a silo franchise and at one point he claimed to have sold every Madison cement silo standing on farms throughout the state of Vermont. By 1960, he had gone into the business of buying and selling used farm machinery. He had also managed to obtain the franchise for Butler steel buildings.

During the middle of the nineteenth century, Addison County was the home of some of the world's best sheep. Most of Australia's merino flock had its origin in some great imported rams that came from Cornwall, Shoreham, and Orwell. But, as Vermont moved toward the start of the twentieth century, agriculture basically changed from sheep to dairy. There were still a few flocks of sheep at the end of World War II. However, by the 1950s, sheep raising had virtually disappeared and did not start to gain ground again until the small mountain dairy farms became uneconomical. As they went out of business, there was a call for diversity in agriculture with less dependency on the dairy industry, and sheep started reappearing.

In the early 1950s, no longer driving a meat cart, Francis was still in the business of buying and selling livestock. After a couple of drinks, Francis would reveal some of his secrets on buying lambs profitably.

On one occasion he arrived at a farm in Orwell, where there was a nice crop of lambs the farmer wanted to market. Francis had agreed to buy them at so much per pound live weight. The way to get an accurate weight is to first weigh the person who is going to lift the lamb onto a scale, in this case Francis, and then weigh him again, holding each lamb. The total weight is recorded and then the weight of Francis O'Brien is subtracted, yielding you the weight of the lamb. This is a better method of finding the lamb's actual weight than trying to put a lamb onto a scale as it is bouncing around.

Francis weighed in and started to lift himself and each of the one hundred lambs he was buying onto the scale. The weight was recorded and he would load the lamb into his truck. Francis started to work up a sweat, and after the tenth lamb, he took off his hat. It had been a chilly early morning so Francis had worn a heavy coat. After the twenty-third lamb, sweating more profusely, he took off his coat and hung it on the edge of his truck. He continued to lift the balance of the one hundred lambs onto the scale, the weight of each being recorded after deducting Francis's weight. The total weight of all the lambs was tallied up, Francis gave the farmer a check, put on his coat and hat, and drove off to the slaughterhouse.

A few days later Francis got a letter from the farmer requesting additional monies due. The letter read, "Dear Francis, When you weighed my lambs the other day, I noticed you took your hat off after the tenth lamb. I calculate the hat weighs about a half pound. I also noticed that after the twenty-third lamb, you took off your coat. I figure the coat weighs about three pounds. You therefore owe me for an additional two hundred and seventy-six pounds of lamb, calculated at ninety at one-half pound for the hat, and seventy-seven at three pounds for the coat. I would appreciate your check and look forward to doing business with you again next year." Francis paid.

It came time to buy the same farmer's lambs the next year. Francis went by the farm the night before they were to be weighed and noticed the lambs out in a fresh alfalfa patch. According to Francis, it was the farmer's intention to have the lambs gorge themselves on the fresh alfalfa, thus increasing their weight by a couple of pounds each. Francis, deciding that he still wanted the lambs and not wanting to try to renegotiate the price, decided on a technique of his own. He put two one pound lead weights in his pants pockets. He then went through the ritual of being weighed in, but this time in deference to the farmer's letter of last year, he took off his hat and jacket before being weighed.

As he was placing the third lamb into his truck, he took one of the lead weights out of his pocket and hid it under the hay at the front of the truck. As he was putting the tenth lamb into the truck, he took the other weight out of his pocket but dropped it. The farmer quickly said "What was that?" Francis went down to his knees and said, "I just sprained my ankle." He successfully hid the second weight and feigned a limp for the rest of the afternoon. He figured that the two pounds gained in weighing each lamb after removing the lead weights just about evened out the two pounds the farmer made by bloating the sheep with fresh alfalfa.

Francis often breakfasted at the Park Diner at the top of Merchants Row in Middlebury, where people would approach him about buying a freezer lamb. One time Don Benjamin approached Francis and asked him what it would cost him to get half a lamb. Francis gave him a per pound price, and Don said that sounded way too much. Francis considered a minute and said, "You want just a half a lamb?" Don said, "Yes." He said, "Well, I can sell you half a lamb," and cut his price considerably. Don agreed. A week later, Francis delivered the box containing half a lamb all freezer wrapped, and picked up his check. Three days later they met again at breakfast time at the diner. Don approached Francis and said, "Francis, in that half a lamb you sold me, there wasn't a leg roast." Francis looked at him and said, "You never asked me which half of the lamb you were buying, and at the price you paid, you only got the front half."

Francis bought a pig farm in Fairfield. He had a hired man run it for him. He had made a deal with two of the local slaughterhouses to take away their unusable offal which he was going to use to feed the hogs. Pigs will do well on just about every type of food and the protein of rich offal was great for fattening hogs. The only problem was that the State of Vermont Department of Health required that the offal be cooked prior to being fed to the pigs to prevent passage of trichinosis or other pig diseases. Cooking was expensive, not only because it was labor intensive, but because of the cost of the fuel oil to flame the furnace. While all the offal did go through the cooking pans prior to it being fed to the hogs, Francis was convinced the hogs liked their offal very rare.

In 1967, fresh out of the University of Michigan Law School, Marshall Eddy became an associate with our firm. A few years later he gave up the practice of law to follow his natural inclinations as a teacher. Sam Morse, superintendent of schools, had the good sense to obtain a waiver for Marshall's lack of teaching credentials and hired him to teach social studies at Middlebury Union High School. He later moved to chair the art department at the high school, where he has become one of those legendary teachers who make school have real significance for its students.

Marshall and his young family had purchased a home in Whiting, a small farming community just south of Cornwall, which is adjacent to Middlebury. Whiting had never had a resident lawyer, and Marshall soon became the lawyer of choice for the residents of Whiting and neighboring Cornwall.

Late one day, just about closing time at his office, Marshall got a phone call from his neighbor, Leona Dapsis. She asked him if he would stop by on his way home. Marshall indicated that he would do so, but not sensing any particular need or urgency, he finished up some matters at the office before he left.

Joe and Leona Dapsis lived on a small farm in Whiting, and while they no longer had a dairy herd, they still kept a few farm animals. Carl Odell was a farmer who lived across Whiting's northerly boundary in the town of Cornwall. He had a small dairy herd and was an active farmer. One of the Dapsises' heifers had calved, and they placed it temporarily in Odell's herd where it could be milked regularly. A dispute arose over the terms under which Odell was caring for the Dapsises' cow, and on a late summer afternoon in 1969, Leona

Dapsis went to the Odell farm to discuss their future relationship with regard to this particular cow.

When Marshall arrived at the Dapsises' home, Leona told the following story: She had gone to the Odell farm to make arrangements to get her cow back. Carl was in the barn and she went there to talk to him. The conversation about the cow became more heated, and finally Leona said, "Carl Odell, you're not worth as much as that cow dung there in the gutter." Carl then reached into the gutter and picked up a fresh cow pie and said, "I ought to push this right in your face." Leona said, "I dare you to." Carl countered, "I really ought to do it." Leona responded with, "I double dare you." At this point, Carl took the fresh cow dung, much like in a Marx Brothers movie, and pushed it right into her face. In resisting his advance, all two hundred pounds of Leona slipped into the manure gutter, causing her to badly sprain her ankle. She managed to get up, get herself to her car, and drive home, and then make a call to the state police before calling Marshall.

Marshall noticed that Leona's face was covered with red blotches, and upon inquiry as to the blotching, Leona said, "Well, I left the dung on there for the state police to see, and I thought you'd be along sooner to see it, but I finally had to wash it off." It was the dung that left the blotches. Marshall suggested that she get some treatment for her injured ankle but told her he could not represent her as Carl Odell was a client of his as well.

When Marshall finally made it home, there was a call waiting for him. It was from Carl Odell. Marshall, knowing he could not represent either party, thought he might be of some use as a peacemaker between two neighbors, so he went over to the Odell farm. Carl related basically the same story as Leona had told him. When Marshall inquired of Carl, "Why did you push that cow pie in Leona's face?" His response was, "I had to — she double dared me."

Marshall's services as a peacemaker were unsuccessful. Leona hired Wynn Underwood, a Middlebury attorney, who later served on the Vermont Supreme Court, and Carl hired Jack Conley. All attempts to negotiate a settlement failed and the case came before the Addison Superior Court at the courthouse in Middlebury for a jury trial. The story of what had happened had made its rounds through every country store, garage, eating place, and bar in Addison County, so when the time came for a trial, the back benches of the courtroom were filled with curious spectators.

This was one of those cases where the economics of lawyering and trials were overcome by the strong emotions of both parties, Leona feeling that she had been wronged, and Carl Odell feeling that he had only done what he had to, given the fact that he was double dared. The trial was in January of 1970, and on the second day the case was settled by a small sum of money being paid to Leona.

I am not sure in today's crowded courtroom schedules whether any judge would be very sympathetic about allowing a matter like this actually to go all the way to a jury trial. However, this trial took place in 1970, and no one thought twice about the propriety of this dispute being resolved in a packed courtroom by a jury of twelve people of the county.

By far the greatest bulk of Vermont farming involves animals rather than cash crops. Even non-traditional farm animals can create unexpected problems. There was the case of the chocolate-loving bunny rabbit.

A young couple had acquired a rabbit as a pet for their children. The rabbit was kept in a cage in the house, and it was the children's responsibility to care for it. This seemed to offer a benevolent experience, and one which would encourage the children of the household to take on responsibilities and also to learn the joys of having a live soft and cuddly pet. The rabbit was treated with affection by the family, and from time to time was fed morsels not only of rabbit food but of chocolate. The rabbit took a liking to the chocolate.

One day a good friend of the family arrived with her two-year old boy for a visit. While the mothers were talking, the child was given a chocolate cookie. As with most two-year olds, not all the chocolate from the cookie went into the mouth but some remained on his fingers. The child noticed the bunny rabbit and decided he wanted to pet it. He reached up into the cage with his chocolate-covered hand, and the rabbit, being more interested in food than affection, mistook the child's finger for a morsel of chocolate, a treat to his diet.

Unfortunately, the way a rabbit eats is to chomp rather than lick, and as the rabbit started to eat the chocolate from the child's finger, it got more than both bargained for. The rabbit chomped down on the child's finger, causing nerve damage. Both the owner of the rabbit and the child's mother might have been more careful in letting the two-year-old approach the rabbit's cage, but one hardly expects a bunny rabbit to be capable of doing damage to a young child. One thing can be said for sure, it wasn't the child's fault in wanting to pet the bunny rabbit and for not knowing the rabbit liked chocolate. Fortunately for all concerned, the owner of the rabbit had a homeowner's insurance policy that paid the medical bills. The child, after some extensive surgery, recovered full use of the finger, and the mothers are still friends.

14.
McIntosh Apples

The Champlain Valley is known worldwide for producing the world's best McIntosh apples. The Shoreham Co-Operative Apple Producers Association is the largest apple co-op east of the Mississippi River. It was established shortly after World War II by a group of farmers under the guidance of Jack Norinsburg for the purpose of helping local orchards market their crop. The Federal Land Bank financed the building of a large storage facility in Shoreham. As years went by, rooms were added, whose atmosphere is controlled so apples are stored in a sealed room having an oxygen-free environment and at a constant temperature of thirty-three degrees. When the rooms were first built, the oxygen was depleted by the use of propane burners and later by the injection of nitrogen gas into the room. The ripening of the apples depletes the small amount of oxygen that is left in the sealed room, and the apples, in the words of the trade, are "put to sleep" in an atmosphere of nitrogen and carbon dioxide. The regular cold-storage rooms are packed out first, and usually in the late winter or early spring the storage rooms having controlled atmosphere are opened and the apples taken from them are sent to market in almost as fresh a condition as if they had come directly from the tree.

Jack Norinsburg not only founded the Co-Op, but he was the chief marketing agent for the apples, selling through his company which operated out of Hunts Point Terminal in New York City. He was also an orchardist and put together a large acreage of producing trees known as Cornwall Orchards. The Shoreham Co-Op could handle 500,000 boxes of apples a year, and when it was at full operation, it employed fifty persons to run the storage facility and operate the packing line.

When the Co-Op began its operation, apples were picked from the trees and placed in boxes known as eastern apple boxes, each holding 1⅛ bushels. As time went on, these were replaced by fifteen-box bins. The packing line, which was the state of the art of the late 40s, continued in operation until 1993, when the directors recognized the equipment had become obsolete. The Shoreham Co-Op directors, looking toward the future, came to the conclusion it was not economically sound to purchase the machinery for a new packing line. Thus, while the storage function continues, the packing has been transferred to Vermont Apple, a packing facility in southeastern Vermont. The apples the Co-Op handled each year at its peak represented about half of the entire crop for the State of Vermont.

In the late 1940s and early 1950s, Vermont was an agricultural state comprised mainly of relatively small family farms. Many of these farmers were looking for ways to increase their cash flow and welcomed the opportunity to pick apples during late September and early October. But, by the late 1950s and early 1960s, the agricultural situation had changed substantially. The number of family farms had declined. The surviving farms got larger and required more attention. Other forms of non-farm employment increased in the area, all adding to the difficulties the orchardists were having in finding adequate harvest labor. There never was a problem getting apples off the trees — nature took care of that — the problem was getting them into the boxes and bins.

During World War II, the U.S. government had started the H-2 Program under which workers from the British West Indies were brought into the United States to supplement a work force depleted by the great need for personnel in both the Armed Forces and the industries supporting the war effort. Workers from the West Indies, primarily Jamaica, came to the United States to do a variety of jobs, including the harvesting of crops. By the late 1950s it was apparent that local labor in Vermont was inadequate to harvest the apple crop. At the same time the crop was also increasing in size because of additional plantings.

The Shoreham Co-Op and its orchardist members turned to the H-2 Jamaican program to find its harvest labor. This program is substantially different from the *braceros* program on the west coast. That program, basically for Mexican laborers, contained many abuses, and rightfully fell in disfavor with the American public. In contrast, the Jamaicans were flown to Miami and bused to Vermont for the six-week picking season. Their transportation was paid for by the growers and they lived in free housing that had to meet federal government requirements. They were paid reasonably well, and by Jamaican standards they could earn enough in the six-week period to equal the average yearly per capita income in Jamaica. The workers, having little in the way of personal expenses, could save their wages, sometimes buying a large array of goods to take back to Jamaica. This opportunity for the Jamaican workers was seen by them as a major help in building up their own small farms in rural Jamaica. The same men would come back year after year, and a trusting and close relationship grew between the growers and these workers. In some cases, the men came back to the same farm for a period of more than thirty years.

When orchardist Bo Patterson's wife, Lois, died, Bo had one of the workers flown up to Vermont to attend the funeral and to read a psalm. At the funeral, the worker told a story about the first year he had come to Vermont. He had torn his pants on the trip north. Mrs. Patterson noticed the tear and offered to repair it. The next day when he arrived at the farmhouse, he found her ironing his repaired pants. He became a part of the family, watching the Patterson children mature, seeing them each harvest season.

The program is supervised by the Central Labour Organisation of the British West Indies. They provide liaison officers who coordinate the transportation of the workers and are on hand in Vermont to see to the workers' needs and to act as a responsible voice on their behalf. The liaison officer for Vermont for many years was Earl Whyte. Earl is a big man who looks more like a linebacker for the New England Patriots than a labor leader. In fact, my youngest son, Eric, thought he was Rosie Grier when he first met him. Despite his size, he was both gentle and sensitive. The workers trusted him and he was able to solve problems before they got started. In more than the forty years of the program, there was never a serious encounter between any worker and Vermont's law enforcement community. It was such a well-run operation, George Meany, one of this country's great labor leaders, actively supported it, even though it brought foreign labor into the United States. He recognized the fact that for every hour of picking time, it required five hours of domestic labor to grow, pack, and sell the apples.

During the same period the sugar industry in Florida was growing and in need of more cane cutters. They participated in the H-2 Program as well. As time went on, many of the workers who picked apples went south after the harvest to cut sugar cane in Florida. Coordination between the Vermont orchard employers and the sugar companies in Florida developed and the cost of bringing the workers from Jamaica was shared.

Over time, the procedures for getting the workers to the United States became more difficult. Each worker had to have individually approved papers from the Bureau of Immigration and Naturalization Service, and that approval had to be based upon a recommendation of the Department of Labor. This required a formal finding by the Department of Labor that there was insufficient domestic labor available to pick the apple crop. This was not politically popular in times of high domestic unemployment.

In 1976, the Department of Labor became more hesitant to certify the growers' needs and attempted to have the growers find their harvest labor from among the ranks of the unemployed. While in theory the numbers indicated that there were sufficient domestic workers available to pick the crop, in reality there was not a competent domestic work force willing to accomplish the task. Here began a long series of legal battles between the Department of Labor, the migrant legal service division of the Legal Services Corporation, and the growers.

In the late summer of 1976, the Department of Labor threatened to refuse certification of the need for foreign workers to harvest the crop. The Shoreham Co-Op sought our firm's help to take on the legal responsibilities of ensuring that the growers would get their Jamaican workers. A meeting was held at the Co-Op, and U.S. Senator Robert Stafford came out to Shoreham to meet with the growers. With his help, they were able to get their labor certification for 1976.

In the spring of 1977, persons within the Department of Labor were beginning to start a crusade to end the Jamaican program. The department made a finding that the prevailing wage rate for picking apples in Vermont (a figure all growers would have to meet in the coming year) was almost double what the growers had been paying Jamaicans. In calculating that rate, they used figures from across Vermont that excluded all the major orchardists who were using Jamaican workers. Their statistics were based on small orchards which were picking only a few hundred boxes of apples for sale at their farm stands. These small orchardists were able to get sufficient local help by paying a much higher per box picking rate. They could afford to do this as they avoided all the additional costs of transportation and housing, and had only a small number of boxes to pick, which they sold at retail.

Bo Patterson became the lead orchardist in a suit brought in U.S. District Court in Burlington against the secretary of labor, calling for a recalculation of the prevailing wage rate. This was critical to the growers, because in order to obtain certification, they needed approval from the Department of Labor. Before the Department of Labor would approve any Jamaicans, the growers had to put into the unemployment system a "job order" testing the availability of domestic workers, and that job order had to contain the prevailing wage rate. That same job order formed the basis for employing Jamaicans, and if the original calculation stood, it would have doubled the cost of wages to the orchardists and would have destroyed the viability of the orchards. There was a second problem. Because of the higher per box picking rate, there might be a large number of domestic responses from people either unqualified or unwilling to really do the work. The growers were convinced that a reliable domestic picking force no longer existed that could and would actually harvest the full crop of apples. We had a young lawyer in our office, fresh out of the University of Pennsylvania Law School, Ellen Mercer Fallon. Despite a tight time schedule, Ellen was able to put together a brilliant legal analysis of the applicable law. Judge Coffrin sided with the growers and they got through the 1977 harvest season.

An Aside

In 1977 there were very few women members of the Vermont Bar, and even fewer who went to court. Ellen later became the first woman president of the Vermont Bar

Association, and on leave of absence from our firm served for two years as legal counsel to Vermont's only woman governor, Madeleine Kunin. A far cry from today where incoming bar classes are almost equally divided on gender lines, and not only are women in court as advocates, many are sitting on the bench, including two of the five justices on the Vermont Supreme Court.

In 1978, the Department of Labor took the position that there were sufficient unemployed Vermonters to fill the three hundred picking jobs usually filled by Jamaican workers. Vermont Legal Aid sided with the Department of Labor and put pressure on the growers to make a full campaign to hire Vermonters to pick the crop. The growers agreed to make every effort, but with the understanding that if the local labor supply did not materialize, the certification would go through and the growers would be able to have their regular Jamaican pickers back and on time. Over the summer, Vermont's Department of Employment Security sent out more than 40,000 postcards to persons who had been on the unemployment roll. The growers advertised in every major newspaper in the state. Toward the end of August, the growers held clinics around the state showing prospective workers the type of ladders they would be expected to climb and the equipment they would have to use. All unemployment offices' potential workers receiving checks were told to show up at those clinics. One day in late August, a ladder was put up in a tree near the unemployment office on Pearl Street. This tree was between the unemployment office and the district courthouse, immediately outside Judge Costello's chambers. I was there because I had been participating in some of the gatherings at the unemployment security offices to make sure the growers were doing in good faith everything the Department of Labor and Vermont Legal Aid wanted them to do. I took the opportunity to climb the ladder up to the level where I could look into the court house and waive at Judge Costello in his chambers. The surprised look on his face when he saw me through the window, perched on a ladder in a tree, is something I'll always remember.

The end result of the postcards, the advertising, and the clinics was that there were approximately seven hundred people who expressed an interest in the work. Of these, three hundred and sixty were referred to the orchards by the unemployment office. Forty-one showed up.

Mike Lipson, the attorney in charge of the project for Legal Aid, worked with us. When it became apparent that we were not going to be able to get Vermont workers to pick the crop, Mike and Vermont Legal Aid cooperated in getting certifications approved, and the Jamaican workers arrived in time to get the work done. While all domestic workers who wanted to pick apples still had their jobs, in the whole state only four of those who had been referred by the recruitment process completed the season. In future years, Vermont was one of the few areas in the country that did not have a running feud with Legal Aid. The growers had cooperated with them in good faith, trying to get a domestic workforce, and when it became clear the apples were not going to be picked by local workers, Vermont Legal Aid decided their resources could be better spent on some other battle. It never gave the Vermont growers a hard time after that.

The U.S. Department of Labor was undaunted. It challenged the growers' practice of advancing to the workers the upward bound cost of their transportation from Jamaica. Under law, the workers who completed the first half of their contract were entitled to be repaid for the cost of their trip north. Those who completed the entire season were entitled to reimbursement for their return home. The Department of Labor took the position that if the growers were going to pay in advance for the transportation of foreign workers, they would have to do the same for domestic workers. This meant that any potential domestic crew who applied for the upward bound transportation would receive the sum in advance from the Vermont growers. The problem was, after they received the money there was never any guarantee they would use it for transportation and actually show up. In fact, in most cases where this was tried, a full crew never did show, and those who did lasted only a few days. To the growers, more important even than losing the cost of the transportation north was the fact they might not have a crew in time to pick their harvest.

A McIntosh apple is more fragile than an egg. It should be picked within ten days of maturity. There is a need for a strong labor force to pick the main harvest within a twenty-day window so that the apples can be placed in storage having controlled atmosphere. That time can be extended slightly in both directions for different varieties of apples and for apples packed and sold that fall. If a McIntosh apple is bruised by being placed too hard in the picking basket, or is cut by the fingernails of a picker, or has a stem pulled from its core, it will not survive as fresh fruit. The cost of picking, transporting, and storage before the damaged apple can be culled is greater than the salvage value of the culled apples, which can only be used for cider. It is better from a financial standpoint for an apple that is bruised or cut to be thrown on the ground to rot, than to be processed through the picking and packing operation only to be culled for cider.

It would appear that picking apples would be rather simple. That is far from the actual truth. Apples, unlike citrus fruit, must be lifted off the tree so the stems come with them. The Jamaicans who came to Vermont over the years had learned this and were capable of picking fruit so well that sometimes ninety-five percent of the apples could be sold for fresh fruit. An inexperienced crew often picked apples in a manner that resulted in a fifty percent culling rate. Thus, careful picking was a matter of survival for the growers.

Starting in the spring of 1977, the Co-Op decided it wanted me to participate in the contract talks that took place each year in Jamaica so I would be fully prepared to deal with whatever legal problems came along in getting the harvest labor to Vermont. As annual certification by the Department of Labor was often delayed until August, or even days before the pickers needed to be in place, they wanted me to be on top of the situation. I was also asked to participate on behalf of the Co-Op in an organization of apple growers along the eastern seaboard, as well as in the meetings of the National Association of Agricultural Employers. At one point the association of apple growers asked if I would be interested in representing all the eastern seaboard growers, but I felt I could not serve both the entire East Coast and my clients in Shoreham, and declined the invitation.

The Shoreham Co-Op orchardists were by far the best agricultural employers of any I ran into. In many other areas there was much less concern for the well-being of the harvest workers and none of the areas had developed the close family relationships that prevailed in Vermont. Having sixteen workers, most of whom came back year after year, living in a summer home on Lake Champlain where they were given free reign to cook for themselves, welcomed back annually by the community and invited to participate in local community and church functions, was in sharp contrast to a labor camp of six to seven hundred workers living in barracks and having to pay for meals supplied by their employers.

In 1978 it became apparent that if we were going to get Jamaican workers to Vermont, we were going to have to find a way around advancing upward bound transportation to potential domestic crews. According to regulations, if we were going to advance the cost of transportation from Jamaica, we were going to have to advance it to domestic workers and provide for that in our "job orders." At a meeting of the National Association of Agricultural Employers, I met with Harold Edwards, the Chief Liaison Officer, and I suggested that the way out of this was to have the Jamaican government, or the Central Labour Organisation of the British West Indies, pay for the workers' upward-bound transportation, and then when the workers had completed half the contract, the growers would reimburse those costs. Harold Edwards finally agreed with my legal opinion, recognizing the seriousness of the situation and the danger to the program as a whole.

I was sent to the annual negotiations between the Central Labour Organisation and the agricultural employers group which were held in Ocho Rios, Jamaica. My job was to try to convince the board of the necessity of undertaking this responsibility.

These meetings were held over a five-day period, and conducted in formal diplomatic style. The first was opened by representatives of both groups making appropriate speeches. There were regular adjournments for purposes of caucusing, and different propositions were put on the table for discussion. By the time things finally got to the table for a vote, all the serious discussions had taken place off the record, and there was little antagonism displayed. Much of the real negotiations took place during a round of receptions or cocktail parties sponsored by the labour board, by the growers, by Air Jamaica, and by Greyhound or Trailways bus companies. For many of the orchardists the meeting was an excuse for a vacation. While I enjoyed it, it was far from a vacation.

Harold Edwards and I had our work cut out for us. We had to convince the Central Labour Organisation or the Government of Jamaica to take on the responsibility for the initial transportation costs for a total of some four to five thousand workers for the harvest labor program. If we failed, the H-2 program was in real legal trouble; and from the growers' standpoint much of the crop would be lost. Each morning we would meet on the beach of the Shaw Park Hotel and swim out to where the cool, fresh water coming out of the hills of Jamaica by way of the White River met with the warm salt water of the Caribbean. It was like swimming through a marble cake as the waters mixed. We could talk privately as we swam and we would plan our approaches to our respective clients for that day. We finally succeeded in convincing the government of Jamaica to take on this responsibility. The growers made some compromises in agreeing to reimburse the government for the upward-bound transportation of workers when they had completed just fifteen days of work. This got the money to Jamaica in time for them to pay the bills to Air Jamaica and the bus companies without having to dip into their very limited foreign currency reserves. Their only real risk was the cost of the workers who would skip and not fulfill their contract, and past experience showed this risk to be minimal.

This procedure worked for just one year before the Department of Labor changed its regulations and said that an advance by a foreign government of transportation costs was the equivalent of the employer advancing costs directly to the worker. This meant that if we expected to continue in our "job orders" to have the domestic workers pay their own way up, then the individual Jamaican workers would have to pay their own transportation costs as well. The problem was that virtually none of the Jamaican workers would be able to raise funds to pay for the upward bound transportation.

Once again, Harold Edwards and I put our heads together and came up with the idea that perhaps we could convince the banks in Jamaica to make loans to individual workers for the cost of their north bound transportation based upon their employment contract. We could then have the workers direct the orchardist to have the banks reimbursed directly for the transportation costs as soon as they complete fifteen days of work. While we felt this would meet the requirements of the Department of Labor, we knew we had a job to do to convince independent banks to make loans to some five thousand harvest workers who had non-existent credit ratings. It would require the banks to assume the responsibility for non-payment of those loans taken out by workers who skipped the job before fulfilling the fifteen day working requirement. Past history had shown that the number of workers who skipped in this period was very small, less than one percent of the entire labor force.

At a meeting of the growers, there was a suggestion that the growers put together a fund to reimburse the banks for losses caused by Jamaican workers who might skip. I said that was out of the question, as it would destroy our position that the banks were really taking a legitimate business risk. Some growers suggested that a fund could be set up in Jamaica for this purpose and no one would have to know about it. I vetoed this proposition as it would amount to trying surreptitiously to get around the regulations of the Department of Labor. It later turned out it was a very good thing that my advice was followed.

The banks would be allowed to charge each worker a small fee that would cover the interest and cost of the paperwork. With this in mind, I went to Jamaica. Harold Edwards and I met with Ken Rattri, the Attorney General of Jamaica, to discuss our approach. We convinced Rattri that this was the only way we could meet the requirements of the regulations of the U.S. Department of Labor. The program was an important source of foreign currency to Jamaica and Rattri recognized the importance of making it work. Together Edwards, Rattri, and I went to the banks. We were first met with an air of disbelief when we suggested they should make some five thousand individual loans to farm works who had no credit history whatsoever. As time went on, we explained to them how the logistics could be handled, that the risk they were taking was minimal, and that they could actually make a small profit, while at the same time ensuring the continued flow of foreign currency into Jamaica. After much consulting with the Central Labour Organisation and with the Jamaican government, they finally decided to give the program a try. The logistics and paperwork were put into place, and the workers traveled north to harvest the crop.

This was not the end of the story. The Department of Labor was convinced, based upon its experience of working with millions of migrant workers over the years, that in no way could there be legitimate loans made to workers on the strength of their employment contract. They believed there had to be a hitch somewhere. A federal grand jury was convened in Boston, and subpoenas were issued to the Shoreham Co-Op as well as to other growers along the eastern coast to testify before the grand jury. Subpoenas also went to the Central Labour Organisation, which, as a matter of principle, fought the subpoenas on the grounds of diplomatic immunity, They were successful in having them quashed. The growers were the only ones on the potential hot seat.

I went to Boston along with employees of the Shoreham Co-op

and we brought out records of the grand jury. By the time the U.S. Attorney's Office, through its grand jury investigation, reviewed all the documentation, they came to realize the entire risk was on the banks and that the growers had not advanced the transportation in any way and had, in fact, only agreed to reimburse the workers for their upward-bound transportation after they had completed the fifteen days of work. This was the same policy they were willing to follow with domestic workers, all as set out in the "job orders."

Had the growers set up a secret fund in Jamaica to guarantee the banks against any losses, there might well have been criminal indictments handed down. I was mighty glad I had insisted upon this being a very real transaction with all the risks being borne directly by the bank. The banks' charge of fifteen dollars per worker to cover their interest expenses, logistics and paperwork of the loans, was reasonable and one beyond the control of the growers. This turned out to be the last major attack by the Department of Labor on the H-2 Program. The program continues to this day in that same format.

I consider this to be the most significant legal accomplishment of my career. It also gave me opportunities that few country lawyers ever have. During the formal negotiations in 1982, the growers were invited to a state dinner at King's house in Kingston by the governor general of Jamaica, His Excellency the Most Honorable Florizel Gladspole. My sixteen-year-old daughter, Katie, had accompanied me to Jamaica as a special treat to us both, and she was included in the invitation. It was rather special to go through the reception line introducing her to Mr. Governor General, Mr. Ambassador, Mr. Chairman, and on into the formal gardens of King's house with a military band playing and waiters serving trays of drinks and food. This was followed by a formal dinner with seating carefully arranged, Katie sitting next to a handsome young lieutenant in the Jamaican Army on the other side of the giant horseshoe-shaped banquet table. After dinner our glasses were charged and a toast was made to the queen. Only then was the great humidor of fine Jamaican cigars I had been eyeing passed around.

Several years later Harold Edwards reached the mandatory retirement age and a party was given in his honor at the Annual Meeting of the Central Labour Organisation and the growers in Ocho Rios, Jamaica. As a result of his work with the H-2 Program, he had been awarded the honors of a Commander Of The British Empire. He was not through, however, as he was hired on as a consultant for another year. At the annual meeting the next year, the chairman of the Central Labour Board held a luncheon, and once again Harold Edwards, C.B.E. was honored. At the cocktail party prior to the luncheon, Harold approached me and asked if I would say the benediction. Harold was a devout Roman Catholic. He knew well that my associations with a church were substantially fewer than his. I suggested to him that there were several other growers who would make a better choice for giving a benediction. I went on to enjoy the cocktail party, thinking no more of his request. As people were seated in the beautiful dining room of the Shaw Park Hotel in Ocho Rios overlooking the magic waters of the Caribbean, Tony Irons, the Chair of the Central Labour Board, took the podium. He announced, much to my surprise, that Peter Langrock would be giving the benediction. I had no choice but to rise and move to the podium thinking quickly what I might say that would be appropriate. As I passed Harold Edwards at the head table on the way to the podium, he looked at me and smiled, and said, "A parting shot."

15.

POTPOURRI

Demonstrative evidence can be invaluable in explaining a situation to a judge or a jury. However, one has to be exceptionally careful in its preparation, as occasionally it can backfire.

I was representing a man charged with possession of marijuana before the district court in White River Junction. The hearing was held in the old district courtroom in the converted post office in downtown White River Junction. That was before the new courthouse was built across the railroad tracks.

The client, driving his automobile, was stopped by a deputy sheriff investigating a possible deer jacking. At the stop, the officer claimed to have seen some red stains, which he thought might be deer blood, on the trunk of my client's car. He requested the trunk be opened, and my client, knowing that he had nothing to do with any deer, complied with the request. When the trunk opened, there was no sign of any deer, but the officer noted a bundle wrapped in heavy green plastic bags. The officer seized the package, unwrapped it, and found a sizeable quantity of marijuana.

I filed a motion to prevent the marijuana that had been seized from being used as evidence on the ground that, while my client had voluntarily opened his trunk, the officer had no reasonable basis to suspect that the wrapped bundle contained marijuana. At the hearing on the motion, which started late in the morning, the state called the deputy sheriff to the stand. He testified that in fact he did have reason to seize the package, as he could smell marijuana when he opened the trunk. I was convinced he was stretching the truth and that he could not have smelled the marijuana as it was tightly wrapped in an impervious plastic wrap. As we approached the noon hour and broke for lunch, the officer was still on the stand. The judge told me to report back at one thirty for my cross-examination.

During the noon hour, I decided to come up with a demonstration I was sure would conclusively prove the officer could not have actually smelled marijuana. Without proof of the smell from the trunk of the car, the officer would have had no right to seize the package, and with this evidence suppressed, the state would have to dismiss the charge.

I went to the local Grand Union and bought a large jar of oregano and a package of heavy-duty locking plastic bags. I took these out to my car and put a sizeable quantity of the oregano into one of the bags, zip locked the bag, and carefully sniffed the bag to determine if I could smell any oregano. There was no odor coming from the bag and my confidence level increased almost to a point of cockiness. The plastic bag filled with oregano went into my briefcase. Looking forward to the cross-examination, I planned to show the officer the baggie and ask him if he could determine visually what type of leafy substance it contained. He would then be asked if he could identify the substance in the closed baggie by its smell, which, according to my previous sniff test, should produce a clear "No" as the answer. When he was asked to open the bag and was finally able to smell the oregano, there was the expectation that he would be surprised and that this would undercut his testimony about the marijuana.

At one thirty the court was back in session. As the proceeding resumed, the briefcase was on the counsel table. I started my cross-examination and in anticipation of using the demonstrative evidence waiting in my closed briefcase, I opened it. Immediately there arose the aroma of a pizza factory. My experiment was doomed to failure. I quickly closed the briefcase, and pursued another line of questioning. Suddenly, around the courtroom, several people were sniffing, trying to figure out the source of a familiar but unusual smell, unusual at least for a courtroom.

A lesson was learned: the locking baggies we use every day in our homes for storing food in our refrigerators are not capable of containing the aroma of strong herbs. The lesson came just in time to prevent me from making a complete ass of myself. If the oregano smell could penetrate the plastic baggie in the time of a lunch break, the argument that the officer could not smell the marijuana because the smell would have been contained within the plastic was out the window. Luckily enough, the briefcase was made of leather sufficiently thick that the smell did not escape through it, but you could be damned sure it didn't get opened again until long after the courtroom proceedings were over. We eventually worked out a plea agreement with the State whereby the client escaped a jail sentence, but I never had the courage to tell him of my failed experiment. The remaining oregano made it onto our spice shelf at home. I love to cook and every time I open a jar of oregano to flavor tomato sauce, the memory of my failed experiment flashes back to me.

Hyde Park is the county seat for Lamoille County. The courthouse and the old jail are on the west side of the one street leading through the village. My client, Johannes von Trapp, and I were heading to court for a round in the Von Trapp family feud, a fight over the value of the stock of the Trapp Family Lodge corporation, and were approaching the courthouse from the north going by the row of big old houses located on the main street. Johannes told me a story of an event he claimed had occurred in one of those houses. Further inquiry showed the story to be true, but the location was wrong. It actually happened in the town of North Troy, which is located twenty-five miles to the north in Orleans County. The lore that evolves out of a courthouse often involves the foibles of people who never quite get to court. Such was the case here:

Around the turn of the last century a rather well-to-do family in North Troy by the name of Currier had decided to leave the cold of the north for the winter months and head south. They decided that this was a perfect time to have the inside of their house redone and have it entirely painted. There was no Home Depot and a painter was expected to mix his own paints and apply them with a brush. The Curriers hired a man by the name of Fred Potter to do the painting. Fred was given directions, a room was made available to him in the basement, and he was given a key to the house so he had the run of the house through the winter. The one thing the Curriers had not counted on was that they had left a cask of a good red wine in the room next to where Mr. Potter was to mix his paints. The Curriers went south and Fred duly started his work. It was not long before he discovered the presence of the cask, and even a shorter time thereafter before he started sampling the wine. Through the course of the winter, the painting progressed well and the wine in the cask kept pace by diminishing at about the same percentage rate as the house was being painted. The wine and the need for Fred Potter's work ran out about the same time.

Fred had no way to replenish the cask and he was concerned about what the Curriers would say when they returned. He formed a plan. He filled the empty wine cask with water, and then carefully lettered on the outside: "Jesus Divine turned water to wine, but I, Fred Potter, turned wine to water."

Vermont is composed of 251 towns and gores, all encompassed within its fourteen counties. A gore is a surveyed piece of land without a sufficient population living within its boundaries to justify a town organization. County governments have little importance in Vermont, but that is not true of towns. Vermonters have always thought of themselves as being citizens of a particular town and are fiercely loyal to that town.

During the 1930s and well into the 1940s almost every town had its own baseball team, and the competition among them was fierce. Towns take great pride in their individual schools, and their town libraries, and often fight at town meeting over the quality of the current road commissioner and his or her maintenance of the town roads.

Kelly James had always considered himself a resident of the town of Weybridge. All of his family for many generations had lived in Weybridge. You can imagine his chagrin when in the 1960s a survey showed that the town line between Weybridge and Cornwall ran directly through his house, with the larger part of the house being located in Cornwall. Both towns wanted their share of Kelly's tax payment, but neither town was particularly excited about taking on the responsibility of educating additional children. Kelly came to see me, and we undertook a search of the law to find where the residence of an individual would be when the town line ran through the house. We found precedents which held that the person was a resident of the town in which the bedroom was located.

On asking Kelly where the town line was in relation to his bedroom, I learned it ran square through the middle of the room. Back to the books. Further research showed that if the town line divided a bedroom, residency attached to the portion of the bedroom in which the homeowner slept.

On being asked where the town line was in respect to the bed, Kelly indicated that the line ran directly through the middle of the bed, halfway between the headboard and the footboard. Back again to the books.

Further research revealed that in the unusual situation we had in hand, you are a resident of the portion of the bedroom in which your head rests at night. I explained the law to Kelly without asking him which way he slept. Whether or not the bed was rearranged by the next day, he called back to assure me that his head, when he was sleeping, was clearly in the town of Weybridge. Kelly James continued to be a resident of the town of Weybridge, and continues to be to this day, running the town meeting as moderator.

Many people think of the practice of law as a sedentary occupation. Ordinarily, a trial is far from that. During the course of a serious trial, counsel must be on their toes one hundred and ten percent of the time. Missing even a single bit of body language from a witness on the stand can be extremely costly to your client. However, there are times when testimony of the other side is more mechanical than substantive, and it is hard to maintain complete concentration. This is especially true at three o'clock in the afternoon on a hot day in a stuffy courtroom. It is not unusual to look at the jury and find some of them listening to the case through closed eyes. Judges have been known to have the same affliction. On some occasions, my chin has involuntarily hit my chest.

Even worse than trying a case through dull testimony late in the afternoon in a stuffy courtroom is defending a deposition on a late afternoon in a stuffy office. Depositions often stretch out merely to authenticate material. Sitting there while the other side is asking your client whether each document from a large stack is actually a genuine document, is not conducive to keeping your mind on the task. Sometimes even large quantities of coffee are not enough to prevent you from roving in your thoughts, and even occasionally dozing.

On one occasion, I was defending the deposition of my client in a divorce case. The part of the deposition that had dealt with the serious matters finished, and opposing counsel continued, verifying a variety of routine, and, quite frankly, dull facts. It was four o'clock on a late August afternoon in our office library. The sun was streaming through the windows and it was in the nineties outside, and not much better inside. Try as I might, my mind kept drifting from the case at hand, and every so often, I would find myself nodding and dozing off. I do not think I actually started to snore, but I can't say for sure. We finished the deposition about five o'clock, opposing counsel left, and I was there in the library alone with my client. He looked at me and said, "Pete, I really don't mind the fact that you were dozing through much of the deposition this afternoon, but I have one question. Are you going to charge me for the time that you were asleep?"

In today's sophisticated world of DNA testing we often forget there was a time when paternity was decided by holding a baby up to the jury and saying, "Doesn't it look like the defendant?" Even into the Twentieth Century when blood tests became common, juries would not always accept their results. Modern blood tests, done correctly, can often establish paternity well beyond the ninety-ninth percentile. In the 1950s, however, blood tests were not that sophisticated and were often used to exclude paternity, but seldom used to prove paternity. A blood test could positively show that a man was not the biological father of the child, but it could not show that the man was the father.

A 1954 case came out of Addison County and went to the Vermont Supreme Court. A young woman had brought a bastardy action, as it was then termed, charging a young man she had been dating as the father of her child. Apparently the defendant in the case was not the only person who had had access to her charms, and thus the case went to the jury to determine whether in fact the defendant was the father. The defendant had been able to obtain blood tests of the mother and child, and, taken together with his own blood test, they showed the mother and putative father both had type "O" blood, but the child had type "B" blood. Scientifically, this ruled out the defendant as being the father.

When the trial judge was asked to direct a verdict in favor of the defendant based upon the uncontradicted scientific evidence, the judge responded by indicating that the blood tests were simply pieces of evidence that the jury could believe or disbelieve. By whatever process of reasoning, the jury came to the conclusion that the father had played the game, they really didn't care which sperm reached the egg first, and the child would be better off being supported by a father than by the town. A cynic might say they concluded there was somebody they could hang it on and save the town from paying various expenses in connection with the birth and care of the child.

The case was appealed to the Vermont Supreme Court, and in their wisdom they agreed with the trial court concluding:

> ". . . We cannot say that the jury were manifestly wrong in rejecting the expert's testimony as to the accuracy of the blood tests that were made."[12]

So much for scientific evidence if the child looks like the putative father.

Rumpole of the Bailey, created by John Mortimer, is an English barrister well known to Americans, both through Mortimer's books and through the TV series. One of the joys of reading Rumpole, or seeing the TV series, is that Rumpole often deals with an underclass in defending members of a family in repeated brushes with the law. These people are portrayed as genuine human beings with a great sense of humor and a balanced approach to life, but, alas, having a rather different approach to what is commonly accepted as morally correct. Unlike Robin Hood, they don't take from the rich to provide for the poor, they instead take from whomever they can, to provide for themselves. A lawyer with a criminal defense practice will over the years represent people of a similar ilk. These are relatively easy clients to deal with as they don't necessarily expect fantastic results. What they want is loyal representation. They have entered into various activities with full knowledge they are breaking the law, and they have made calculations on a cost-benefit analysis of what their chances are of getting away with it and what the risks are if they are caught.

Vermont has had on its books since 1927 a law allowing for the prosecution as habitual offenders of individuals who have already been convicted of three felonies. The habitual offender statute carries with it possible life imprisonment. The idea behind the habitual-offender statute is to get career criminals off the street. However, it applies equally to people who rob banks on a regular basis and those who cash bad checks on a regular basis. Historically, it has been used infrequently, and often it has been applied in situations where the activities of the defendant are a continuing thorn in the system, rather than a source of real danger to the community.

Robert I. Tepper was state's attorney of Rutland County in 1970 when Raymond Leslie Rushford, with a record of thirty-two felony convictions, was once again charged with a series of counts involving both writing bad checks and burglaries. The grand jury indicted him as a habitual offender.

The first count Rushford was indicted on was a charge of passing a bad check at a service station. As Bob Tepper was preparing the case to go to trial, he interviewed the witness who had identified Rushford as the perpetrator. When asked how he could identify Rushford, he told Tepper that it was easy — Rushford had a gold tooth. Tepper, in an abundance of caution, called the state prison where Rushford was being held in an attempt to verify that he indeed had a gold tooth. The warden, Robert Smith, replying to Tepper's inquiry, said, "That's funny, he went to see the prison dentist last week and had his gold tooth removed." Realizing that might put a small crimp in his presentation of the evidence, Tepper decided instead to go forward on the second count, the burglary of a small pizza parlor. Here, Tepper had a stronger case. A companion who had participated in the burglary had turned state's evidence and was going to act on behalf of the state as a snitch in return for limiting his own sentence to three years.

A trial of a criminal case is more than a simple presentation of the evidence — it's a production, much like a live play. It requires timing in its presentation, as well as enough pizazz to keep it interesting and to make the jury sensitive to the full nature of the case. Part of this can include highlighting the effect on the victim. Bob decided to call Ted Vignoe, the owner of the pizza parlor, as a witness to describe what had been taken from the premises and how it affected him. He did this to humanize the proceeding even though he believed the testimony would have little direct evidentiary value as to the guilt or innocence of Mr. Rushford.

The owner was called to the stand and duly sworn. After the preliminary questions he was asked what he noticed when he returned to his store after the burglary. He was a dignified Italian-American who spoke with an accent. "It was a mess. He took everything. He took my pepperoni. He took my provolone cheese. He took my lucky one-dollar bill — the first dollar I got when I opened the pizza parlor." Then, after looking directly at the defendant, he quickly turned to Judge Franklin Billings and said, "Hey Judge, Mr. Rushford, he's wearing my shoes." This totally unexpected piece of evidence brought laughter to the courtroom and sealed the conviction of Mr. Rushford. The supreme court subsequently affirmed his conviction.[13] You sometimes wonder whether a defendant like this simply wants to go back to jail.

16.
THE LITMUS TEST

Becky Durenleau was married to Mike Durenleau and they lived in Swanton with their children. Becky was having an affair with Harmon Olmstead. On the 12th day of July, 1985, at about 9:00 p.m., Becky and her husband Mike went to Victoria's Place, a bar in Essex Junction, and parked their car to the rear of the building, close to the railroad tracks that run through the village. They went into the bar and ordered beers. Mike went back to get something from the car. When he hadn't come back for several minutes, Becky went out to look for him. What she saw was somebody running away and her husband lying on the ground. He had been stabbed in the heart. The police were immediately called and an investigation commenced. It was clear Becky had no direct involvement in the killing, but as the investigation went on, her affair with Harmon Olmstead was discovered. He became a suspect of having actually done the killing. The police looked at Becky as possibly having set up her husband for Harmon to kill. This would constitute the crime of being an accessory before the fact and would carry the same penalty as murder itself. Suspicion circled around Harmon, but the investigation never revealed any direct evidence tying him to the homicide.

John Powell was the owner of Flanders Lumber Yard, which was separated from Victoria's Place by a railroad spur. He was sitting in his vehicle, parked just down the road, keeping a sharp eye out, because he was worried about potential thefts from his lumber yard. He noticed a pickup truck pulling into the parking lot in front of his store. It moved out of his line of vision and he drove over to investigate. He found the truck parked, but with no sign of the driver, and, after checking his store, he went home. Later, when he heard about the killing, he called the police and told them about the truck and also that he had seen a man walking from the parking lot toward the railroad tracks. While he could identify the make and model of the truck, he wasn't sure of its color, and he had not taken down the license plate number. The model of the truck turned out to be the same as one owned by Olmstead.

Harmon Olmstead was never indicted. Some six years after Mike Durenleau's death, Bill Sorrell, then the state's attorney of Chittenden County, decided to reopen the case. He presented it to a grand jury, which returned an indictment against Becky Durenleau, charging her with aiding and abetting Harmon Olmstead in the killing of her husband. The grand jury did not indict Harmon Olmstead himself. It later appeared that the true purpose of Sorrell's obtaining the indictment against Becky was to scare her into turning state's evidence against Harmon Olmstead, who the state believed to be the true culprit. Becky had been represented by Mike McGinn, a St. Albans attorney, who contacted me. I interviewed Becky who told me that she had nothing to do with the killing and asked me to represent her at the upcoming trial. I agreed to do so. During the course of preparing for trial, I became convinced she was telling the truth. Her children, who had lost their father in the tragic occurrence, supported their mother one hundred percent.

What often happens in the investigation of a serious crime is that once the police have a serious suspect, and Harmon could obviously be considered as such, they tend to look only for evidence that supports their theory while disregarding any evidence suggesting other possibilities. It is an occupational hazard and probably results in more convictions of innocent people than any other police practice.

In this case, Becky's attempt to put forward a defense was made even more difficult, because a substantial body of evidence that might have proven her innocence was now seven years old. One might think that a seven-year lapse in bringing a case would make it harder for the state to prove the guilt of the accused beyond a reasonable doubt. In actuality, the opposite is true. Witnesses tend to remember the thrust of incriminating evidence, and their details start to fit the theory more and more as their memories of the context of what happened fade. This is exactly what occurred in Becky's case.

By the time we got to trial, the state had been able to gather small pieces of evidence that directed suspicion at Becky, but had not come up with a single piece of hard evidence pointing toward guilt. They could show that life insurance on her husband Mike had been increased shortly before his death, although admittedly this was brought about by the initiation of the life insurance salesperson. They could show that she was having an affair with Harmon and was considering leaving Mike to be with him. They concluded that she thought she would be better off with her husband dead than having to go through a divorce.

The state also came up with a woman as witness who claimed that she overheard Becky say on the phone to Harmon prior to Mike's murder that Harmon would have to "prove himself." The witness further testified that, at some time subsequent to the murder, she was present when there was another phone conversation between Becky and Harmon, in which Harmon had said, according to Becky, "Have I proven myself now?" The state, with no more evidence of context than that, came to the conclusion that the conversations must have reference to her desire to have her husband killed, and Harmon's admission that he had accomplished the act. Matthew Katz was the trial judge, and it was this one statement that he said was enough to tie Becky sufficiently to the case and let it go to the jury.

The state's case was: Becky was a fallen woman whose financial situation would be better off with her husband dead; she had driven with her husband to the place where he was killed; the place was not one they usually went to; and there were the ambiguous statements about Harmon having to prove himself, and later having done so.

The defense of the case had two major problems. One was a body of evidence that in my mind established her innocence but was inadmissible. The second problem was Becky herself. Becky was a warm, affable individual who loved to talk. The problem was, her love of talking was greater than her memory. If you asked her what she did yesterday, she would tell you elaborately what happened, and then if you asked her the same question twenty minutes later, she would give you a repetition of what happened the day before, but with significantly different details. In the course of the investigation, she had given statements to the police, and while none of these incriminated her in any way, there were discrepancies in what she told the police at different times. It would be virtually impossible to put her on the stand, as there was no way she could consistently explain those differences without looking as if she was lying and making things up. That would have been deadly to her defense.

The state's theory about exactly how the killing happened was never consistent, and it even changed from time to time. Curiously enough, the knife Mike was killed with was his own and had been in their car. This was at least inconsistent with the idea this had been a pre-planned murder. The state's theory also varied from whether it was done by Harmon Olmstead alone, or whether it was done by two or more people. A bloody hand print on the car proved to be that of someone other than Harmon Olmstead, and shoe prints at the scene were never tied to Harmon's shoes.

One of the things that convinced me of Becky's innocence was the fact that two days after the homicide, she took a lie detector exam by submitting to a polygraph, at the state police headquarters. The person who gave the polygraph concluded she was telling the truth when she said she had no knowledge of the murder. Subsequently, another examiner read the charts of the polygraph and came to the conclusion that, contrary to the first examiner's determination, the results were inconclusive. Ordinarily, if Becky had had any knowledge at all of the actual homicide, the polygraph charts would have jumped all over the place, and it would have been clear to the first examiner that she was lying. Seven years later when we were preparing for trial, we tried to obtain the original charts of the polygraph so that they could be read by an independent examiner on our behalf. For the first and only time in state-police history, these charts were missing, apparently stolen from the state police headquarters. No one could explain where they were. It was useless to run a test some seven years later. So much had gone on, the blending of fact, suspicion, and worry, along with the anxiety over the pending charges, would have made the polygraph an unreliable instrument for getting at the truth. It was not unreliable two days after the killing when Becky took, and apparently passed, the test. Unfortunately, none of that information was available to the jury.

During the course of discovery, another interesting fact came to light. The entire investigatory file of the Essex Police Department, the chief investigating body of this homicide, had been taken to the dump and destroyed. Thus, all that was available to us was a reconstructed file rather than the original one. A further complication came in the form of information not made available to us in the course of discovery, which we learned about for the first time at trial. Eleanor McQuillen, the state pathologist who had done the autopsy, kept certain notes which had not been turned over to us. In the course of her testimony, I received these notes and found that she had made reference to an ax handle the police had seized as a potential murder weapon. This was important as the deceased had been stuck with a blunt instrument, as well as stabbed. Upon further inquiry, we found in fact that an ax handle had been taken into possession by the Essex Police, but again for some unknown reason, that piece of evidence had been checked out of the evidence locker and destroyed. There was no explanation offered as to why the original file was destroyed, or why the alleged murder weapon had been removed from the evidence locker and destroyed.

Another body of evidence which was not allowed to be presented to the jury concerned a recorded phone conversation between the investigating officers and the FBI. In that conversation, the FBI suggested that the investigating officers set up the following scenario: The investigators create false evidence implicating Becky, put it in a file, and invite Becky and her attorney to meet with them. They then leave Becky and her attorney in a room with the file containing the false evidence. The FBI further suggested that defense counsel would take the opportunity to look through the file and would become convinced that the state had a stronger case than it had. They could use that impression as leverage to get Becky to point the finger at Harmon Olmstead. They further threatened Becky with the loss of her children as a method of putting pressure on her. The inappropriateness of these tactics would have supported our contention that what we had here was a mere gathering of facts pointing to a preconceived theory, rather than an objective, impartial investigation.

It took a week to try the case, which was covered live and broadcast nationally by Court TV. The case was argued and given to the jury on a Saturday. They had not reached a verdict by Saturday night. The jurors, who had been going home each night of the trial, were now kept together and put up in a hotel. Sunday morning they attended a religious service together, after which they continued deliberations, and late that morning they brought back a verdict. When the foreperson announced that the jury found the defendant guilty, Becky fainted in her chair and fell to the floor. The rescue squad was called. She was being given emergency first-aid as the jury was polled individually. After the jury was discharged, Becky was taken to a hospital where she was held under guard.

Becky was devastated. I was in a state of shock. It is not easy for a lawyer to hear a verdict of guilty of a charge of first degree murder when the lawyer knows in his heart the person had nothing to do with the murder. The only hope was an appeal.

An appeal was taken. Each area where we felt the trial court had made erroneous rulings was carefully spelled out in the brief we filed with the court. The principal argument of the brief was that there was simply not sufficient evidence which would allow a jury to find Becky Durenleau guilty of first degree murder on the facts before them. The state had, in effect, admitted as much by not seeking an indictment of Harmon Olmstead. They admitted they did not have sufficient evidence to prove the homicide against the person they believed committed it, and the only additional evidence they had against Becky was the statement that Becky had allegedly made to Harmon that he would have to "prove himself." This statement had been admitted into evidence without any contextual background concerning it. The case was argued before the full supreme court, and again Court TV was present to broadcast the arguments. Court TV subsequently ran a program entitled, "An Anatomy Of An Appeal" in which they showed excerpts from the appeal, discussed the issues, and had commentators reflecting on the possibilities of success. One commentator thought Becky had a good chance on appeal, but doubted the supreme court would decide on an outright acquittal, which is what we had asked for. Several months went by during which time Becky was incarcerated at the Chittenden County Correctional Facility in South Burlington.

It is not often that the supreme court hands down a decision which overrules the trial court in a criminal case and enters an outright acquittal. Ordinarily, at best, all a defendant can hope for is a new trial. In this case, the supreme court analyzed the evidence and unanimously came to the conclusion that a jury cannot convict somebody of first degree murder based solely on evidence of suspicion. I received a call the morning of September 30, 1994 that the supreme court had rendered its decision, and had in fact reversed the jury verdict. It was with great pleasure I called Becky at the prison and gave her the news. I talked with Scot Kline, who since the trial had taken over as state's attorney, and he agreed he would not object to her immediate release, even though he was planning to file a motion for reargument. I told Becky I would meet her at the jail at three o'clock. She was ready to go, and she walked out a free woman with the remaining inmates at the windows cheering her on. It took a long time for justice to triumph, and the time Becky had unjustly spent in jail was lost to her forever, without any recompense.

Another frustrating aspect of the resolution of this case was that shortly after the trial, Governor Howard Dean had taken Bill Sorrell from his state's attorney position and appointed him director of administration (and later failed in an attempt to have him appointed chief justice of the Vermont Supreme Court), and then adopted this case as his "litmus test" for judicial appointments. Without any real knowledge of the case or the background of it, Dean decided that the supreme court's decision was a miscarriage of justice. One can perhaps understand Bill Sorrell's belief in the rightness of the conviction, seeing that he was an advocate, and obviously had convinced himself that Becky was guilty or he would not have brought the case. However, for a governor to condemn a decision without a real understanding of the process involved, without looking at both sides of the issue, but accepting only the position of the prosecutor does not speak well for the separation of powers in Vermont. Dean stated publicly that he only wanted to appoint judges who would have upheld the conviction of Becky Durenleau and that this case was his "litmus test" for the appointment of judges.

Brian Joyce and Joseph Carroll of WCAX-TV in Burlington were given the prestigious Silver Gavel Award from the American Bar Association for their five-part series, Judging Justice. That series focused on the working of the Vermont Supreme Court, and especially zeroed in on Governor Dean's criticism of the Durenleau opinion.

In referring to aspirations of John Dooley and James Morse to be appointed chief justices, Brian Joyce led the following dialogue:

> Joyce: But their decision in the Durenleau case may have ruled them out.
>
> Governor Howard Dean: Sure. I ask about that when I make appointments.
>
> Joyce: You asked about Durenleau?
>
> Dean: I asked about Durenleau.
>
> Joyce: What did you ask?
>
> Dean: I asked if it's proper to throw out the evidence that a jury has heard that led to a conviction.

So much for a politician's understanding of the significance of due process and the need for an independent judiciary.

17.

A GREEK TRAGEDY

In the early spring of 1966, my office phone rang. I picked it up and my secretary told me that Franklin County Sheriff John Fenn, a good Democrat and, more important, a good man, wanted to speak to me. A call from him was always welcomed. I hardly expected the drama that would unfold as I answered, "John, what can I do for you?" He responded that he had a young man in the Franklin County Jail by the name of David Gibson, who wanted to talk to me. I asked him, "What's the charge?" The answer, "First degree murder."

I had never handled a murder case before, even as a prosecutor, and the adrenalin started flowing immediately. Sheriff Fenn put my potential client on the phone, and I told him not to talk to anybody about anything until I got there, and that I would not be long. I told my secretary I was off to St. Albans and didn't know when I would be back, and would she please cancel the appointments for the day. It didn't take me much over an hour to cover the sixty miles to St. Albans, and miraculously I got there without being stopped for speeding.

The old jail was located in a red brick building behind the courthouse. The jail building housed the sheriff's office and had a few small cells that were typical of the county lockups of the day. John Fenn ushered me into a room in the sheriff's offices and then brought in my client. David Gibson was sixteen years old, red-haired, and had a face full of freckles accented by a broken front tooth. He stood about 5'6" tall. He was hardly the picture of who you would expect to see when you first meet a person charged with murder.

Young Gibson told the following story. David and his brother John had arrived home late from visiting some neighbors. Their father, Herman Gibson, was in a rage and he yelled at both boys. John, who was the younger brother, didn't respond exactly as his father wanted him to, so his father grabbed him, threw him to his knees, putting the boy's head between his own knees, and started pounding on the back. As John cried out, David moved quickly to the other side of the room, grabbed a four-ten gauge shotgun from a shelf, pointed it at his father and yelled, "Leave my brother alone." His father let go of John and came at David saying, "Why, you little son of a bitch, put that gun down." David retreated to the wall, and as he backed up, the gun went off, killing his father.

The father had a reputation as an abusive individual. Just the week before when the boys had come home late, he took their pet beagle out to the back of the house and shot it dead, just to teach them a lesson.

It appeared to me that the state, at best, had a case of manslaughter and not of murder. Even more important, David had the potential defense of justifiable homicide. When a killing takes place while a person is trying to protect either himself or a family member, it can be justified as either self defense or defense of another.

The first legal step was in municipal court before Judge Carl Gregg. Gregg would hear evidence to determine whether my client should be bound over to the superior court for a grand jury proceeding. I had some hope that at this hearing we could eliminate the charge of murder and have David face a grand jury proceeding only on a charge of manslaughter. However, Judge Carl Gregg had a penchant for favoring the state and I was not optimistic that this would actually happen.

In a binding-over proceeding the judge is asked to decide that there is sufficient evidence to have the defendant held until a grand jury can consider whether or not an indictment is to be returned. Ordinarily, at the hearing the state puts on its case giving a brief outline of the facts in order to establish probable cause. Usually, that is the end of it.

I had just finished reading a Perry Mason novel which involved a binding-over procedure. In the book, Perry Mason called a witness on behalf of the defense at the hearing. To my knowledge this had not been done in Vermont, but I thought I would give it a try. Bill Goldsbury, who was the state's attorney, made his presentation, and as he concluded the court indicated it was prepared to make its finding. I interrupted, and without citing Perry Mason as my authority, said I wanted to call a witness. I argued that additional information certainly couldn't hurt the proceeding, and Judge Gregg reluctantly allowed me to call my witness.

I called David's brother, John, to the stand. John related the entire incident: he was being beaten by his father, his brother, David, warning his father to leave him alone, then David retreating as his father went after him, and finally the gun going off killing his father. John also testified that just the week before the father had shot and killed the boys' pet beagle as punishment for their coming home late. I knew the press was going to be there and I wanted to get our side of the story out as soon as possible. John's testimony apparently made a much smaller impression upon Judge Gregg than it did upon the local papers. He rendered a decision binding David over to the grand jury on the first degree murder charge. However, the overall strategy worked, as the newspaper featured John's testimony, and a few days later when the grand jury met, they returned an indictment on the lesser charge of manslaughter.

Shortly after the indictment was returned, David was brought from jail to be formally arraigned on the manslaughter indictment. He pled not guilty, and as the charge was now manslaughter and not first degree murder, it was appropriate to set bail. State's Attorney Goldsbury and I conferred about setting bail. We agreed that given David's age, it would be best not to keep him in jail, but to have him released in the custody of a responsible adult, in this case his grandmother. Superior Judge Rudolph J. Daley was presiding and he called us back into chambers to discuss the bail situation. Judge Daley had one major failing: he really didn't like to make decisions. Further, brought up in the old school, he was very reluctant to let anyone be released on any charge without cash bail. Goldsbury and I suggested that he could set an amount of cash bail and let the grandmother sign a bond without having to actually raise the cash. He finally agreed on the amount of thirty-five hundred dollars, but wasn't sure that he wanted to allow the grandmother to act as surety rather than requiring her to post cash. Cash was not readily available and David would have had to go back to jail.

Suddenly, as if a light bulb went on in Judge Daley's mind, he said, "I only have to set the amount of the bail. It's up to the clerk to decide what he will take as a surety." Jay Chaffee, who was approaching eighty, was the county clerk. Chaffee immediately began to shake and stutter, not wanting that responsibility at all. Finally, after the state's attorney and I once again argued that jail was no place for this sixteen-year-old, Daley agreed that bail set at thirty-five hundred dollars could be satisfied by David's grandmother signing for it. She would also have custody of David until the trial.

Attorney General John Connarn (later a district judge) entered his appearance to assist Bill Goldsbury with the trial. When the case came up for trial in the summer of 1967, it was held at the Franklin County Courthouse on the east side of the city park in St. Albans. The trial itself was straightforward and the evidence for the state went in easily. Every time I got the chance, I examined witnesses about the killing of the beagle by the father the week before the incident. That theme was reiterated often enough that one spectator quipped at me at a recess, "Are we trying the murder of Herman Gibson or of the beagle?" The state rested its case, and my motions for dismissal were denied.

Now came the defense's turn to put on its case. I called David Gibson to the stand. It was the first time his version of what happened would be heard in public. Bill Goldsbury and John Connarn were poised to take extensive notes in preparing for cross-examination. I asked David just four questions. The first was, "What is your name?" The second, "Have you listened to the evidence and your brother's recitation of what happened, and is it basically true?" He responded that it was. The next question was, "Did you intend to kill your father?" He said, "No." The fourth and final question was, "How did you feel about your father?" He asked, "What do you mean?" I reiterated, "Well, how did you feel about him?" He said, with his eyes getting misty, "I loved him."

"No more questions." Goldsbury and Connarn had not even started to take notes and were completely surprised by the length of the examination. Connarn got up to do a cross-examination, and after a few disjointed inquiries, he sat down. The defense rested.

The time came for closing arguments, and John Connarn led off. He recited the facts surrounding the killing, and as he got to the point where John was being held by his father and David went to get the gun, he added that David reached into his pocket, took out a cartridge, and loaded the gun before pointing it at his father. This latter statement was made from whole cloth as there was not a scintilla of evidence about the loading of the gun.

I had to make the quick choice of whether to object right then and there or wait until the argument was finished. An objection would call the jury's attention to Connarn's statement and emphasize it. I decided to sit quietly and try to look completely unruffled, waiting to object until after the attorney general's argument was finished. As Connarn completed his argument, I was on my feet instantly and asked permission to approach the bench. Permission was granted, and in whispers at the bench out of the hearing of the jury, I moved for a mistrial, stating that the state had injected a highly prejudicial conjecture into its closing that was completely unsupported by any evidence in the case. The court denied my motion for mistrial, but asked me if I wanted a corrective instruction that the jury should disregard what the attorney general had said as not being with the evidence. I argued that such an instruction would only call attention to the unwarranted assertion about the loading of the gun and that my client, already prejudiced, would be better off if nothing further was said.

I had always assumed that the gun was loaded before David took it from the shelf, as I had never seen anything to indicate the contrary. Later I decided never to ask David how the gun got loaded.

When the arguments were completed, the judge gave the charge on the law to the jury. He submitted to them my request that they consider that the killing had been justified on the grounds of having been necessary in order to prevent harm to his brother or to defend himself.

In my argument to the jury, I had tried to emphasize the tragedy of it all. I spoke in terms of David not intending to kill his father, a person David loved, despite his faults. While I never specifically used the words "Greek tragedy" in my closing, I hoped to invoke just that image. The *Boston Globe* in its coverage of the case indicated that the defense argument was a comparison of it to a Greek tragedy. The jury was out for about two hours and returned a verdict of not guilty.

After the case was over, I filed my petition for attorney's fees with the court, as I had been assigned to represent David at state expense. Assigned counsel at that time were paid by the state at a rate of fifteen dollars per day for investigation and twenty-five dollars per day for trial. In serious cases, the court was allowed to make an additional award of attorney's fees for what was called "argument." This was the factor that would allow defense counsel in serious cases to receive something more than the minuscule payments provided by the state. Often a sum of five hundred dollars or more was allowed. Judge Daley, after hearing my request for attorney's fees, stated that he was upset that the young man had gotten away with killing his father, and awarded me a sum of only fifty dollars for "argument." While the cash flow to the office from the case was negative, the acquittal, with the attendant publicity, more than paid its way in establishing my credibility as a criminal-defense counsel.

That was the story as I had remembered it after more than three decades. I checked with my former client, David, because even though the facts were in the common domain and I was not breaching any client confidences, I would not include the story in the book if it would cause David any discomfort. He voiced no objection and forwarded the draft I had sent him to his brother John. John wrote the following letter which says so much more than I remembered:

Dear Peter,

I don't recall how much information was ever divulged to you about what led up to the shooting of my father, but there was a lot. For now I will focus on the six pages that you sent my brother and give you what I recall (vividly) about those issues.

David is slightly less than 5'4" *not* 5'6".

David and I had *not* returned late from visiting neighbors. My father had kept me out of school to work on the farm. He had also done this the previous year which caused me to fail the seventh grade. David had already quit school in the seventh grade and had work papers to allow him to do so.

Because of my frustration, I told my father that since he was keeping me out of school again and I would probably be kept back again, I chose not to go back to school at all. My father was not the kind of man that you said no to. After having been physically and verbally abused since I was around 7 years old I knew what to expect. I had determined that I would not give in this time. I had actually decided to die rather than live under the conditions I had been living under. My father had beaten me for quite some time, all the while my brother David and sister Kathy begged me to give in so my father would stop. I would not. I wanted to die. Finally, my mother went to bed. She was always too afraid to help or say anything for fear of being beaten herself.

My father had also begun drinking which made him uglier. David and I were the only two left in the room with him. Me being abused and David made to stay and watch. It finally escalated to me staring at my father in defiance and him knocking me down and kicking me as I crawled under the table trying to escape. He grabbed me by the legs and dragged me back all the while beating me to the point of exhaustion for him and me.

As I was crawling toward the table a second time with my father stomping me with his foot, I heard David say, "Leave John alone!" The rest of what you've stated about that is correct.

The dog that my father shot was a mutt not a beagle. A pregnant stray dog had come to our farm and had a litter of puppies. We hid this from my father for weeks knowing that he would shoot them. When he finally found out he did shoot all but one of them. The one left was my favorite which I had named Mr. Mutt. I loved that dog more than anything. My father knew this and when I would not give in to his demands earlier that fateful day, he brought me and Mr. Mutt to the garden and said that if I did not do as he said that he would shoot Mr. Mutt. I would not give in and he shot Mr. Mutt. I was then told to dig a deep hole and bury him then I was left alone to do so. I cried terribly over that dog and the guilt I felt for causing his death. That is where the line was drawn. I did not care anymore. I did not fear anymore. I had given up on my own life.

The rest of what you have written I have very little memory of except, I do recall what was in my opinion a very caring and dedicated request that you made of me. While you were questioning me prior to the trial I kept breaking down and crying. At one point you said to me, that if I wanted to help my brother (which I did) that it would not hurt if I were to cry like that on the stand. I did cry on the stand and it was genuine, while at the same time I understood how it could help my brother.

What you accomplished for us was fair and just. You freed eight children and their mother from a terrible situation which my father brought on himself. There are stories about those years that would shock people and I wish I could tell those who doubted including judges, how wrong they were.

As you know many years have passed, but my father left us with lifetime scars unable to completely heal. When I look back on my life, there are some bright stars and you are certainly one of the most important.

Yours truly,
John G. Gibson

ラリー　エドワーズ，
個人別及び同種の状況下に置かれた他の
者達にかわり，

原告。

18.

ALASKA

In 1971, James Jeffords was Vermont's Attorney General. He
brought a case for the State of Vermont against the State of New
York and International Paper Company directly in the United States
Supreme Court. This suit charged that the sludge bed resulting from
the waste of IP's mill at Ticonderoga Bay[14] was changing the deep
water channel of Lake Champlain. It is the middle of that channel
which marks the boundary between the two states: New York was getting bigger, and Vermont was getting smaller. Starting in 1971 and
continuing through 1989 our office was involved in two civil lawsuits
growing out of the operation of both the old mill at Ticonderoga Bay
and a new supposedly pollution-free mill built on the south lake by
International Paper Company a few miles farther to the north.
Jeffords had promised to make the evidence he had of the pollution
available to our clients, and each succeeding attorney general honored
that promise. These suits pitted Vermont lakeshore owners against IP
as the polluter of Lake Champlain and its environs. In the course of
these suits, I made two trips to the United States Supreme Court.

In the summer of 1990, I met a brilliant young lawyer from

Washington, D.C, Terry Reed. We met in connection with work of the National Conference of Commissioners on Uniform State Laws, where Terry was an advisor from the American Bar Association on the Uniform Controlled Substances Act. His abilities are exceeded only by his determination. When he gets on a case, he is like a pit bull, charging ahead without fear and biting anything that gets in his way. Our styles may have differed, but our philosophies were the same, and we soon became good friends.

Terry represented Ted Seaver, a former employee of Alaska Pulp Company's Sitka, Alaska mill. After he had testified at some congressional hearings in a non-complimentary way as to his employer's environmental practices, Seaver's job was terminated. Of course, APC claimed he had been dismissed for other reasons, and the differing views became the basis for a lawsuit. In the course of working on that lawsuit, Terry became acquainted with several members of the Sitka community who were concerned about the pollution caused by the pulp mill. At one point, the mill was ranked as the fourth worst polluter in the United States. It was located at the inland end of Silver Bay and dumped its effluent into the pristine waters of the Pacific Ocean in Silver Bay. The Sitka residents asked Terry what could be done about it.

Terry, knowing of my role in the litigation against International Paper, approached me to see if there were any effective remedies available to them. It was immediately apparent that these individuals could not possibly put together a war chest to take on the pulp company in proceedings before the Alaskan Environmental Protection Agency. The EPA had the power to order environmental controls, but the cost of producing expert testimony to counter APC's engineers would have been prohibitive. There is only one way to deal with a company like that: go after its pocketbook. They had millions to spend in defense of their way of running the mill. The only potentially effective thing we could do was threaten to make them pay money for the damage they were doing to the environment.

There is an old common law cause of action called "nuisance." The gist of "nuisance" is that a person is responsible to use property in a reasonable way so not as to interfere with the property rights of others. We could allege that the plume of effluent from the APC mill as it was dumped into Silver Bay was affecting the property values of the other owners of shore property. It affected lands right up to and past the city of Sitka itself to the point of land where the waters left the bay and emptied out into the wide Pacific Ocean. Nuisance was the cause of action our office had used successfully against International Paper Company.

Over Labor Day weekend of 1990, my partner, Emily Joselson, went to Sitka to meet with some of the people who had expressed environmental concerns. She reported back that the pollution was considerable, but that the ocean is a big place, and the nuisance case, while legitimate, was a long way from a slam dunk. Later that fall, I went to Sitka and met with these same people to discuss a proposed strategy. Generally, they were in favor of suing APC, but before going forward, they wanted to know what their risks were in case of a loss. In evaluating their question, we ran into the first of many of the quirks of Alaskan law. We were later to learn of the many quirks of Alaskan politics.

Under Alaska law, the winner of a lawsuit is entitled to obtain legal fees from the loser. This is the so-called "English Rule." The "American Rule" is that people ordinarily pay their own legal fees regardless of outcome. Alaska is the only state which has adopted the "English Rule" as its general rule. It was adopted so injured persons would not have to deduct from the monies awarded to them for their injuries to pay attorneys' fees. This put the burden of attorneys' fees on insurance companies or large corporations who could best afford it. Ours was a different situation: we were representing the little people. There was a very real risk that if we lost the case, Alaska Pulp Company would claim several million dollars in legal fees, financially wiping out those persons who dared to bring suit. Despite their strong feelings about the irresponsibility of Alaska Pulp Company and its constant pollution of the waters of Silver Bay, the average homeowner found the risk too great to undertake. Among those wanting to pursue the case, however, was a dedicated environmentalist, Larry Edwards. Larry said he was willing to step up to the plate and risk his entire net worth if the case failed. Larry had a small business in Sitka, selling and renting kayaks. In January of 1991, he took on the responsibility of starting a class action on behalf of all the riparian or waterfront owners of Sitka, as the sole representative of the class.

Ordinarily, when you bring an environmental case against a wealthy and powerfully connected polluter, you find some sympathy within the state agencies which have been trying to regulate the pollution. Initially, that was true in the APC case, but soon politics cut off any help we were going to get in that regard. We had enlisted the help of the Alaska law firm of Robinson, Deiswenger & Ehrhardt, who had been involved on behalf of plaintiffs in previous cases of environmental litigation, notably the Glacier Bay oil spill and the Exxon Valdez oil spill. We also got the help of a sole practitioner from Sitka, James McGowan, who felt strongly enough about the pollution to take on the case, in spite of the fact that much of his practice depended directly or indirectly upon the economic benefits the mill brought to Sitka.

Coming from the East Coast, both Terry Reed and I envisioned Alaska as the last great wilderness and assumed the residents of the state would be environmentally sensitive and would want to protect their beautiful state from pollution. We learned the opposite was true. Alaska, because of its great natural resources and their immense value to the rest of the world, had for the most part become governed by people who were interested in making money, even at the cost of the environment. The vastness of Alaska contributes to this type of thinking. Even where the pollution was atrocious, as in the APC situation, it was such a small part of a giant panorama that it appeared as only a small blip when compared to the vastness of the state.

We obtained a preliminary ruling that the members of the class who had not signed on as representative parties, that is everybody but Larry Edwards, would not be responsible for legal fees in case we lost. With that ruling in hand we proceeded to send out notification to approximately four hundred landowners who had waterfront property. It was this mailing that brought home to us the reality that Sitka was a very divided town on the question of the mill. With a population of only eighty-five hundred people, the seven hundred employees of the mill directly touched almost half the families in town. Indirectly its economic power went a great deal further. APC put on a public relations campaign, and by the time the date for returning the notices came, almost two-thirds of the landowners had opted out of the lawsuit, saying they did not wish to participate. We still, however, had a viable economic basis for proceeding, and we went forward, engaging experts and preparing the case through extensive pre-trial procedures. Fortunately, we found sympathetic ears within the court system, first in the personage of Judge Walter Carpeneti and then Judge Larry Weeks. Over the next two years I became well acquainted with the

Alaska Airways milk run from Juneau to Sitka to Ketchikan to Seattle and the red-eye back from Seattle to Chicago, connecting to an early morning flight to Burlington.

While the lawsuit was proceeding through the normal discovery procedures, Alaska Pulp Company went to the state legislature. There they lobbied through a bill which outlawed the common law action of nuisance in all cases where an industry was regulated by state environmental agencies. The bill went so far as to be retroactive. In effect, the Alaska legislature had, by legislative fiat, attempted to throw us out of court. Again the judiciary came to our rescue and ruled that the portion of the legislation which acted retroactively was unconstitutional, and as our lawsuit had been filed prior to that legislation, we could go forward with it.

Also, during this period, the Alaska Department of Environmental Conservation, while for political reasons not being able to be of much direct help to us, began to put pressure on APC to clean up its act. To meet their requirements, APC was going to have to expend large sums of money, perhaps in excess of one hundred million dollars. APC decided to close the mill.

Shortly after the closing of the mill, the immense potential of the Pacific Ocean took hold, and where once the water was so discolored by the effluent that you would lose sight of a white disk at the end of the line when it reached the depth of three feet, you could now see many fathoms into the crystal-clear water. There was still the plume of pollutants on the bottom of the bay that would remain there for many years to come, but the immediate dangers to the waterfront property, and even to the fish that traveled through the waters, was drastically reduced. Our lawsuit now dealt only with damages for past effects on our clients' properties and the possibility of punitive damages. Punitive damages would have to be based upon the willfully reckless disregard APC had shown in dealing with the environment in the past.

Throughout this time, both in our lawsuit and before the legislature, APC was crying poor. In fact, APC was an Alaska corporation owned by a Japanese corporation that was owned by four of the major Japanese banks that controlled much of the then healthy Japanese economy. This fact had required us to have the initial court pleadings translated into Japanese so we could bring the Japanese corporation into the jurisdiction of the Alaska courts. We had evidence to indicate that the poverty, as claimed by APC, was simply part and parcel of transfer pricing. They sold the high-grade pulp produced by the mill (used in Japan to manufacture such products as photographic film) to business-related Japanese buyers at cost rather than at an arm's length market value, enabling the profits to be realized in Japan rather than in the United States. They thus avoided both state and federal taxes, and left the operating company in a position to be able to cry poor.

For about one-half of the population of Sitka, the closing of the mill was a very unpopular decision. There were sections of the city, and specifically some bars, where we were labeled as carpetbaggers who had caused the mill to close. Those were places we actually did not dare to visit.

It was also during this period that APC brought in an attorney from San Francisco by the name of Richard Kramer, now a judge, to augment the work that had been done by Jim Stoetzer of the Seattle firm of Lane Powell Spears & Lubersky. Kramer was tough and good.

In the course of our discovery, we learned that shortly before the mill had closed, and while the mill was crying poverty, claiming an inability to meet the demands of the state environmental agencies, its president, George Ishiyama, a native born American of Japanese descent, had been given a twenty-five-million-dollar personal bonus. We thought this an act of arrogance, and one that would possibly anger a jury sufficiently to stimulate a large award of punitive damages.

George Ishiyama turned out to be a very interesting person. During World War II, he and his family had been interned in a camp in Utah pursuant to the infamous order that called for the rounding up of all Japanese-Americans and, despite their U.S. citizenship, seg-regating them as potentially unloyal. After the war, Mr. Ishiyama went to Japan and became the resource adviser to an industrial bank there. Basically, he oversaw the contracts which allowed U.S. iron ore from Utah and other places in the United States to be sent to Japan to help build Japan's steel industry. He became a person of substantial wealth and ended up with large holdings of land and other investments throughout the southern Pacific. He was also a man who was com-fortable either in the setting of American business (he once sat as a director of the Wells Fargo Bank) or in the formal business structure of Japan. The banks who were the ultimate owners of APC had asked Mr. Ishiyama to come out of semi-retirement to take over as president of APC.

We wanted Mr. Ishiyama to appear for a deposition in the United States. By the time of our request, he had returned to Japan and resided permanently in Tokyo. APC resisted our request and we had to go to court to enforce our rights. The court ordered that either Mr. Ishiyama appear in San Francisco or that APC pay for the travel expenses of two of the plaintiffs' lawyers to go to Tokyo to take his deposition there. APC decided on the latter course of action, and in January of 1993, Terry Reed and I made preparations to go to Tokyo.

Terry had been to Tokyo previously, when his brother lived there. I left making the arrangements of the trip to him. We were to meet in Newark to board a United Airlines 747 for a direct flight to Tokyo. The weather was a bit iffy, so I opted to fly to Newark the night before. On the day of our flight, Newark Airport was in the middle of a snowstorm. As the flight to Tokyo was a major source of revenue to United Airlines, if there was one flight that day that was going to get out of Newark, it was going to be our flight. Terry was flying in from Washington that morning, and the weather was causing all sorts of delays on local flights. The time came to board the flight to Japan, and all I had learned about Terry's location at that point was that he was somewhere in the air trying to land at Newark. I boarded the flight and realized that I was off to Tokyo with no knowledge of the hotel we were staying at, no knowledge of the overall setting, and unable to speak a word of Japanese. Our flight was delayed in taking off because of the weather, and by some small miracle, about two minutes before departure, the door opened and Terry appeared. Needless to say, I was glad to see him and, while long, it turned out to be a pleasant flight.

Before going to Tokyo, I had visited with a former secretary of mine who had taught English in Japan. My son, Fritz, had spent some time studying Japanese culture and had suggested some reading concerning Japanese customs. This preparation served me well in the long run. Among the things I learned was that the Japanese treasure business cards very highly. It is the custom when meeting someone to present your business card, which card is looked at carefully and acknowledged with formality. I also learned that the Japanese custom of gift giving is an integral part of their culture. The third thing I learned was that the Japanese do not, in their business transactions, deal with confrontation lightly. The confrontation that American lawyers deal with regularly in our adversary system is simply considered rude and usually turns out to be counterproductive. I was going to Japan for the sole purpose of confronting a president of a Japanese-owned company about why, and under what circumstances, he had taken a personal twenty-five million dollar bonus a few months before the plant had closed. I had to map out a plan to deal with these customs without forfeiting our need for the information Ishiyama would give us.

The day before the deposition was scheduled, Terry and I were walking along a Tokyo street when a jogger appeared from the other direction. As he passed us, he looked, and said, "Pete, Terry." Our surprise at being recognized on the streets of Tokyo was put into perspective when we realized it was Jim Clark, a member of APC's legal team.

The deposition was held in a private room at one of Tokyo's grander hotels. As Terry and I entered the room and met Mr. Ishiyama for the first time, I handed him my card saying, "Here is my card so you'll know which of the devils I am." He smiled politely, took my card, and examined it. I then reached into my briefcase and took out a jug of maple syrup and said, "I bring you a present from my home." This caught him totally off guard. He recognized that I was attempting to take this deposition in a manner respecting Japanese traditions, and not in the confrontational manner of the American adversary system. We started the deposition in a cordial manner, covering the corporate structure and Mr. Ishiyama's background. As we moved toward the key question of the twenty-five million dollar bonus, I showed him a financial report of APC. The report indicated in a footnote that he had in fact received a twenty-five million dollar personal bonus. I asked him if he had read the financial statement. He said that he had not. I then asked him if he would read footnote #4, which contained the information about the bonus. I waited until he completed reading it and then asked him if the information contained in the footnote was true. He responded, "Yes." We had on record all the information we needed. The burden was now on APC to explain the appropriateness of the bonus if they could. This shifting of the burden was accomplished without direct confrontation.

During the rest of that deposition, and a parallel one taken by Terry Reed in the *Seaver* case the next day, I found myself liking Mr. Ishiyama. We had off-the-record conversations about the horrors of the Nisei program which called for the segregation of Japanese-

Americans, and about what was happening in Congress to try to leg-islate some reparative payments. We talked about the American Civil Liberties Union and a variety of other things. At one point his counsel suggested that perhaps he should not be discussing matters with me informally. Mr. Ishiyama overruled his counsel and said he felt quite comfortable talking to me. As we were leaving the room after fin-ishing the deposition, he said to me, "In my travels throughout the world, I have met very few Vermonters." I replied, "That's probably because there are so few of us."

Shortly after the deposition we started some settlement discus-sions in earnest. From our standpoint, much had been accomplished. The mill was closed and the pollution was clearing up. We wanted, if possible, to avoid the expense and risks of a trial. On the other hand, even though the actual damages of the case had been minimized, the defense still had to deal with APC's previous pollution, and its dele-terious effects, and with the reality that, while crying poor, the com-pany had paid its president a twenty-five million-dollar bonus.

Eventually, we agreed on a three-million-dollar settlement, which would pay a million dollars in legal fees, with two million going into a trust. Half of the income from the trust would be used each year in the city of Sitka for special grants for the arts, and the other half would be used to make grants for Sitka High School in the scientific field, with the understanding that all grants would have to be for matters over and above what the normal high school curriculum would pro-vide. The purpose of the latter grant was to enhance the science pro-grams, not to replace public funding of the schools. When we finally presented our proposed settlement to the court, the court appeared moved that we had been able to create a positive result out of a most contentious piece of litigation. The court approved the settlement, and it was eventually approved by the class members, despite a few who thought the monies from the settlement ought to go to them individually. Our response to them was that the acts of the mill in the past had lowered the property values of all of Sitka by its pollution, and that the settlement in this case would increase the property values by making Sitka an even more special place to live.

APC, through its parent corporations, had the resources to push the case to the wall, and the power possibly even to eventually deny payment if we won due to the insolvency of the Alaska Pulp Company itself. The settlement was a very good thing for us and for the people of Sitka. The relationship I had developed with Mr. Ishiyama as a result of respecting his cultural norms played a very important part in our ability to reach a settlement. I was told subsequently that at one point Mr. Ishiyama said to his counsel, "If we settle this matter, is there any way we can get Mr. Langrock paid and none of the other attorneys?"

In a final twist, the unusual Alaskan Rule 82 shifting the burden of paying legal fees was used as a sword against plaintiffs' counsel, limiting the legal fees to five hundred thousand dollars. After an appeal to the Alaska Supreme Court, and a remand from that court, we were awarded fees of seven hundred and fifty thousand dollars, plus expenses. They were shared by all of the plaintiffs' attorneys. Although we never recovered fully for the time we spent, we felt we had made a major contribution to Sitka and to the environmental movement.

LIST OF CASES

1. *State v. Harrington*, 128 Vt. 243 (1969).
2. *U.S. v. Trudo*, 449 F.2d 649 (1971); *U.S. v. Tatro*, 452 F.2d 1207 (1971).
3. *State v. Cabrera*, 127 Vt. 193 (1968); *State v. Barr*, 126 Vt. 112 (1966).
4. *In Re Rich*, 128 Vt. 373 (1966).
5. *MacEdward v. Northern Electric Co., Ltd.*, 595 Fed. 105 (1979).
6. *First Vermont Bank & Trust Co. v. Kalomiris & Thunder Road Enterprises, Inc.*, 138 Vt. 481 (1980).
7. *Lyons v. Bennington College Corp.*, 137 Vt. 135 (1979).
8. *Nichols v. Nichols, Jr.*, 139 Vt. 273 (1981).
9. *State v. Chapman*, 126 Vt. 167 (1966).
10. *State v. Doria*, 135 Vt. 341 (1977).
11. *In Re Shequin*, 131 Vt. 111 (1973).
12. *Pomainville v. Bicknell*, 118 Vt. 328 (1954).
13. *State v. Rushford*, 130 Vt. 504 (1972).
14. *Vermont v. New York*, 417 U.S. 270 (1974).

INDEX